Towards a Philosophy of Caring in Higher Education

Yusef Waghid

Towards a Philosophy of Caring in Higher Education

Pedagogy and Nuances of Care

palgrave
macmillan

Yusef Waghid
Faculty of Education
Stellenbosch University
Cape Town, South Africa

ISBN 978-3-030-03960-8   ISBN 978-3-030-03961-5 (eBook)
https://doi.org/10.1007/978-3-030-03961-5

Library of Congress Control Number: 2018962937

© The Editor(s) (if applicable) and The Author(s), under exclusive licence to Springer Nature Switzerland AG 2019
This work is subject to copyright. All rights are solely and exclusively licensed by the Publisher, whether the whole or part of the material is concerned, specifically the rights of translation, reprinting, reuse of illustrations, recitation, broadcasting, reproduction on microfilms or in any other physical way, and transmission or information storage and retrieval, electronic adaptation, computer software, or by similar or dissimilar methodology now known or hereafter developed.
The use of general descriptive names, registered names, trademarks, service marks, etc. in this publication does not imply, even in the absence of a specific statement, that such names are exempt from the relevant protective laws and regulations and therefore free for general use.
The publisher, the authors and the editors are safe to assume that the advice and information in this book are believed to be true and accurate at the date of publication. Neither the publisher nor the authors or the editors give a warranty, express or implied, with respect to the material contained herein or for any errors or omissions that may have been made. The publisher remains neutral with regard to jurisdictional claims in published maps and institutional affiliations.

Front cover image © Hendri Venter / Getty

This Palgrave Macmillan imprint is published by the registered company Springer Nature Switzerland AG
The registered company address is: Gewerbestrasse 11, 6330 Cham, Switzerland

Foreword

In this new book by Yusef Waghid, *Towards a Philosophy of Caring in Higher Education,* the reader is taken on a *tour d'horizon* through, as Waghid describes, his personal, public and professional sojourns as a philosopher of education. The itinerary of this journey turns attention to key topics in the current debate on education and learning in the arena of higher education, thoroughly exploring what it would mean to speak of a 'caring relationship' between teacher and students, colleagues and academics, and the global and local community. It opens up a wide, yet well-argued and excellently written theoretical landscape. The reader delves into Waghid's rich philosophical expertise in the field of education and learning, linking substantial works of critical pedagogy (Freire) with feminist ethics of care (Noddings) up to an African ethic of *ubuntu* caring as an emancipatory, humanising and politico-pedagogical act, to name but a few.

What makes this book most valuable and refreshing in times of turmoil, be that right-wing parties gaining strength in Europe, political inventions such as 'alternative facts' or the imbalance in academic research standards towards quantitative indicators, are not only the profoundly theoretical, but indeed practical elaborations on how to conceptualise and to enact what Waghid calls 'authentic pedagogical encounters in higher education'. Yusef Waghid does not hesitate to tell about and scrutinise his own experiences as a teacher, supervisor or also editor-in-chief. Thereby, he offers insights into personal challenges, in the value of, in that sense, caring dissonance and in supportive academic infrastructures like the SUNCEP SciMatUS programme at Stellenbosch University that addresses the educational needs of students coming from disadvantaged learning environments. In this way, higher education is contextualised: it is embedded in local histories, cultures and communities, also as part of the wider global frame, and the added value of this contextualisation for teachers and students, institutions and communities is recognised – pointing to initiatives in higher education, which are gathered, world-wide, under the concept of 'service-learning' (see e.g. Pacho, 2018). The latter exemplifies the point that learning cannot be narrowed down to a neuro-psychological behaviour, but there are ethical and political responsibilities under negotiation, questions of equality and social justice, and ideas of humanity deeply ingrained within.

Tying these issues in with the book's key notions of *care* and *rhythm*, Waghid explores a so far rather neglected and unknown terrain in the debate on education and learning of adults. The book argues for a rediscovery, and, in this sense, a rewriting of the idea of care. It liberates this idea from a welfare state's often paternalistic and deficit-oriented attitude towards its citizens (and dis-citizens, as Devlin and Pothier (2006) remind us), and it cancels the traditional pedagogical hierarchy, inscribed in architecture, curricula and relationships, between a supposed learner in need and a designated teacher who shall take care of that need. Waghid makes the point that the notion of care is meant to be seen away from *caring for* and *caring about* others towards *caring with* others – opening up reciprocal processes in pedagogical encounters instead of a pedagogical one-way traffic and a priori fixed roles and responsibilities (of who is meant to care and who is meant to be taken care of). Yet, this is far away from naïve conceptions on harmonising pedagogical encounters, but emphasising, by supporting Cavell's (1997) considerations, the value of ruptured moments of scepticism.

In this sense, Waghid argues for an understanding of a *rhythmic caring*; embodying what he calls 'fluctuations of attachment and detachment', or giving and taking in processes of education and learning. Thus, Waghid urges us to think that rhythmic caring becomes resonant only through mutual relations and back-and-forth fluctuations that allow pedagogical encounters to become more enriching for all those who are involved. Exposing the significance of rhythm as a temporal movement, but also as a subject-related, virtually embodied category in a given society, links the work by Waghid to the current debate on the characteristics of modern societies, also brought forward by Hartmut Rosa (2015), a German sociologist and political scientist. Rosa wishes to identify *social acceleration* as the dominant feature of today's temporal structure of society – lacking relationships of resonance. In discussing such phenomena through the lens of education and learning, the new book by Yusef Waghid provides a vital and much-needed theoretical framework. It opens up an arena for debate, in which the voice of the Swiss psychosociologist Michel Alhadeff-Jones with his work on *Time and the Rhythms of Emancipatory Education* (2016) also needs to be taken into account, echoing Waghid's impetus on the emancipatory potential of education and learning.

Exploring the theoretical frameworks and practicalities of caring, rhythm and pedagogy in higher education and beyond, allows the reader to join this excellent *tour d'horizon* by Yusef Waghid. It pushes the boundaries of thinking and acting in the arena of education and learning and reminds us of their emancipatory potential: an often downplayed, yet, genuine task and most valuable guiding principle of (adult) education.

Hamburg, Germany   Silke Schreiber-Barsch

References

Alhadeff-Jones, M. (2016). *Time and the rhythms of emancipatory education: Rethinking the temporal complexity of self and society.* London: Routledge.
Devlin, R., & Pothier, D. (2006). Introduction: Towards a critical theory of dis-citizenship. In D. Pothier & R. Devlin (Eds.), *Critical disability theory* (pp. 1–22). Vancouver, BC: UBC.
Pacho, T. O. (2018). *Service-learning in higher education in Africa.* Newcastle upon Tyne, UK: Cambridge Scholars.
Rosa, H. (2015). *Social acceleration: A new theory of modernity.* New York: Columbia University Press.

Preface

My own initiation into philosophy of education came about through my engagement with democratic educational theory as a master's student in the late 1980s. Considering that, as a group of eight to ten students, we were recognised as a community of philosophers of education working on educational research projects of common interest. We were privileged to have encountered in person, through seminar presentations organised by the programme leaders, among the most reputable scholars in the field of both philosophy and education. It was at one of such seminars as a master's student, that I encountered in person, Professor Charles Taylor, the Canadian philosopher, whose thoughts on multicultural education and ethics came to influence both my early thinking and writing in and about religious ethics, education and democracy. Taylorian thought introduced me to an understanding of concepts and practices in education and how such an understanding was influenced by the notion of a shared, intersubjective community – that is, how intersubjective action constitutes a sense of community (Taylor, 1985). At a very early age in my academic journey, Taylor's ideas on intersubjectivity and community therefore influenced my thinking to the extent that I authored a thesis on teacher evaluation in relation to the idea of a democratic, intersubjective community (Waghid, 1992). Yet, without making too much of the idea of caring at the time, it was always a practice implicit to my understanding of what it means to engage in an intersubjective community. That is, even as emerging philosophers of education at the time, we thought it apposite to think of ourselves as belonging to a community in association through our subjectivities, prepared to disagree, yet having remained cognisant of the *caring* relationships we have fostered through our mutual actions. It was, therefore, not uncommon even for one of my classmates, Sue Soal, to have produced a thesis on caring and education. Unwittingly, Sue in listening to her arguments, introduced me to the work of Nel Noddings. In fact, what interested me even more at the time was that Sue was not only relying on Noddings's caring framework for her thesis, but she was also prepared to take issue with some of Noddings's claims on caring. Nevertheless, through my own engagement with the seminal thoughts of Charles Taylor, in particular my understanding of his concept of intersubjectivity, I encountered, for the first time, Noddings's book on caring and education. Not only was I a member of an intersubjective philosophy of education community in my early years as a master's student, but I was also privileged to have encountered works of care as embodied through the writings of Taylor and Noddings – by far, two of the theorists whose works fascinated me the most as an emerging philosopher of education. Only in my later years did I actually introduce myself to Nel Noddings at an American Educational Research Association (AERA) conference in Chicago. By then, I was already immersed in my thoughts in and about caring in relation to education.

Strangely enough, despite my early exposure to thinking about care, I never really directed my educational research along the lines of care. Instead, I focused on a concept of community, which nowadays can be couched as a democratic community. My own PhD, which I also completed in philosophy of education, focused mainly on the concept of a democratic community vis-à-vis religious practices within a specific community. Yet, my own doctoral voice in the early 1990s never really abandoned the concept of care (Waghid, 1995). If I were to rephrase my argument in my doctoral studies today, it would invariably be about a defence of community in religious education, more specifically Muslim education, which has the potential to care for those that constitute such a community. Inasmuch as my own doctoral work was a defence of a reconceptualised notion of *madrassa* education, I did not think of such a form of education independent from an ethic of care as espoused by theorists, such as Gilligan (1982) and Noddings (1984) mentioned below. By implication, my early life as a master's and doctoral student can be associated with the idea of an ethics of care that provided the backbone to the ideas that I develop in this book. The point I am making, is that care within education always constituted my engagement with the concept. And, most notably, my enunciation of the concept of relevance to education features most prominently in my work completed in the field of democratic educational theory vis-à-vis notions of an intersubjective and deliberative community.

The question arises: why does this book focus on education, caring and rhythm? Of course, the work of Italian philosopher Giorgio Agamben (1994) was inspirational, especially in relation to my treatment of the notion of rhythmic caring in this book. However, long before Agamben came to reshape my thinking on rhythm, I was already influenced through rhythmic action during my years as a doctoral student. My rigorous and hardworking supervisors, Professors Nelleke Bak, Wally Morrow and Abdul Kader Tayob, deserve much credit for inspiring me through their comments. Not only did they challenge me throughout my writing, but most importantly, they also introduced me to a way of doctoral supervision that relied overwhelmingly on rhythmic assessment. In most cases, their critical and rigorous feedback on drafts of my work seemed at first like a momentous affront. However, when I actually engaged with their criticisms on my drafts, I began to realise – even while I am authoring these sentences now – how they evoked my potentialities in quite a rhythmic fashion: they gave me credit for what they read, but pushed me to think deeper about my research, and, on resubmission, they engaged with my writing in rhythmic fashion once more. Thus, through my learning and writing, I came to experience what it means to be engaged in a pedagogical encounter influenced by rhythm. There is no doubt that my supervisors cared about the scholarship in the making although it seemed, at times, that they cared less about me and more about the scholarship under examination. Of course, they cared, and their caring was one of engaging critically with my writing and provoking me to come up at times with more plausible justifications. The latter understanding of care is quite ambiguous: on the one hand, caring for the ideas espoused in a thesis is a vindication that the rigour of arguments is taken care of. But then, on the other hand, caring for arguments indirectly links to the notion of caring for a student, as arguments are proffered by the student. That is, caring for and about arguments and the person who proffers them, are inextricably intertwined. It would be difficult not to care for a person; yet, caring for the scholarly persuasion of the arguments made by a student.

To my mind, the understanding of care that came to be associated with my doctoral journey was one of push and pull in much the same way Agamben (1994) uses the concept in relation to spontaneous human action that goes through moments of attachment and detachment – that is, encounters of push and pull. It could be that supervisors review a student's arguments and offer evaluative judgements that laud the arguments. Yet, simultaneously they point out the weaknesses in the arguments and, at times, offer ways by which the arguments could be strengthened. Thus, supervisors give advice on the basis of their evaluative judgements of the work they encounter. Likewise, they also appraise some of the arguments in order to encourage a student to continue embarking on the research. In this way, it seems as if using a push-and-pull phenomenon in recognising argumentation is a way of advancing the writing of a thesis. In much the same way, my supervisors seemed to have responded to my work.

Since Nel Noddings's (1984) monumental work on caring in relation to education, the literature on caring in philosophy of education abounds. Yet, it was Carol Gilligan's (1982) contribution to the notion of caring that preceded that of Noddings in the sense that she (Gilligan) argues for caring as a relational human experience that appeals to universal principles of rights, contractual reciprocity and justice (Gilligan, 1982: 74). In other words, caring is a human act of mutuality whereby humans are bound by universal rights of well-being and rationality coupled with an enactment of just and humane practices. Following on such a view of caring, Noddings (1984: 128) extends the afore-mentioned Aristotelian view of caring to educational relations among teachers and students in the sense that teachers care for students when they (teachers) listen and are attentive to them (students). Noddings (2006: 239) further develops this particular view of caring whereby one transcends your individuality to imagine what others experience, that is, one draws yourself into the world of others and begin to make sense of their human experiences.

Much of my work with university students over more than two decades appeals to Noddings's universalist idea of caring to the extent that I consider my pedagogical encounters with students as an act of justice – that is, my engagement with them as carer involves being attentive to their pedagogical concerns with a commitment to their learning becoming authentic. By authentic learning I mean three things: first, students are initiated into pedagogical practices whereby they are encouraged to speak their minds – a matter of coming to speech as Jacques Rancière (1991) posits. Coming to speech implies that students are not just told what to do. Rather, they make sense of what has been articulated by teachers and then autonomously construct their understandings even to the extent that they might want to take issue with what teachers have said. Second, when students make sense of teachers' thoughts, they endeavour to bring that with which they engage into controversy. Similarly, through reading a text, students begin to understand, explain and justify meanings within and beyond the text in a deliberative way. That is, students bring understandings of a text into controversy and in such a way happen to develop more insight into a text by making sense of the text in the light of those thoughts that confront them and with which they engage deliberatively. Third, initiating students into university education is invariably connected to them becoming ethical beings. That is, students do not learn only this or that related to university curricula; more poignantly, they are stimulated to enact change in the communities with which they engage. In other words, teaching – and, by implication, students' learning – is inextricably connected to cultivating and responsive beings. More specifically, my teaching is linked to students enacting their responsibility – that is, they are accountable to the communities with which they engage. They are also responsive to the challenges with which they are confronted, and then endeavour to change distorted or undesirable situations. In this way, they might act ethically whereby ethical pursuits are linked to them (students) engaging in responsible and responsive encounters.

From the afore-mentioned understanding of caring follows that it is a relational human activity, more specifically, pedagogical experience, whereby I have attempted to evoke the self-understandings of students in order that they speak authentically. Put differently, caring is not just about a teacher doing something for a student in the sense that the former cares.

Rather, caring implies that a student does something for him- or herself, such as when he or she makes an autonomous judgement informed by yet independent of a teacher's authority – a matter of a teacher telling the student what to think and say. Of course, there are times when students rely extensively on the views of teachers when they make rational judgements. However, at other times a student might make a judgement independent of a teacher's perspective. Therefore, I would like to introduce an idea of caring whereby a student is being cared for differently in pedagogical encounters. Based on Giorgio Agamben's (1994) notion of rhythm, my argument is that caring involves someone doing something for someone else without hindering the other's response – that is, a matter of offering something as a result of which someone else might initiate an action, such as when a teacher evokes the self-understanding of a student to develop an independent point of view, on the one hand. In other words, in pedagogical encounters, a teacher holds back his or her own judgement about some or other matter in order that the student may develop his or her own rational judgement unconstrained by the teacher's perspective. On the other hand, a teacher attempts to influence a student's perspective by constantly reinforcing his or her views through the proffering of justifiable reasons that might influence the student's point of view. In such a situation, the teacher endeavours to release his or her judgement to the extent that the student's perspective is not entirely his or her own autonomous point of view, but it is partially, and perhaps, at times, largely influenced by the teacher's perspective. Such an act of holding back and releasing one's judgement invariably affects the way in which students proffer their own judgements. Consequently, pedagogical caring can also be rhythmic when the teacher holds back and releases his or her judgements in such a way that students' judgements are influenced accordingly.

Such an understanding of rhythmic caring can most appropriately manifest in pedagogical encounters that allow space for dissonant action: discomfort, practical criticism and scepticism (Davids & Waghid, 2017). The point I am making is that rhythmic caring has the best chance of being realised in an atmosphere of dissonance. For instance, when a teacher holds back his or her judgement about a particular pedagogical matter, he or she creates an opportunity for students to speak their minds in an unconstrained way. This means students do not have to be too concerned when their views are in disagreement with those of fellow students. Their exposure to multiple views stimulates them to reconsider their own judgements in the light of that with which they are confronted, even if it means that their views are perhaps in conflict with those of other students. The point is that the dissent that exists among diverse perspectives offers an opportunity for students to adjust and re-articulate their own views. A teacher responds only when students have concluded their judgements and then willingly articulate their rational formulations in the presence of a teacher and students. Put differently, rhythmic caring allows students to become increasingly willing and confident in articulating their enriched judgements about pedagogical concerns. The point is, students are not prematurely judged and prevented from articulating and re-articulating their understandings. Rather, they are encouraged to speak their minds repeatedly without being prevented by teachers to do so.

Moreover, my reason for coupling care with rhythm, is based on an understanding that caring on its own is an enabling but not a sufficient human value to influence the nature of human encounters, more specifically, pedagogical encounters at universities. In a way, I am therefore advocating for a notion of care that is linked to other values, such as autonomy, justice, mutual respect, democracy and empathy. In other words, I specifically show how other human virtues are implicated in the action of care, in much the same way that Nicki Hedge and Alison Mackenzie (2012: 193) show as how emotions are implicated in the activity of care. Hedge and Mackenzie (2012: 196) argue why sympathy, compassion, empathy, anger, disgust, pity, hatred and justice are 'evaluative judgments that form our emotions, colour our desire and capacity to care'. More poignantly, they show as how 'the emotions [are] implicated in morally appropriate care' (Hedge & Mackenzie, 2012: 196). Pedagogical encounters in higher education that are designed to cultivate transformative human action – as I argue for throughout this book – will require an expanded notion of care, that is, rhythmic care. As I show later on in this book, care is not an absolute concept that does not exist in an extended form in relation to virtues such as empathy and compassion in particular. Although this is primarily a book about care, I also show why and how other virtues, such as empathy and compassion, extend a notion of care.

This book is organised in twelve interrelated chapters in which I address theoretical views on caring in relation to university teaching and learning and, then, examine their implications for a philosophy of higher education in Africa. A coda is included in order to address a central issue of online or digital caring within pedagogical encounters.

Chapter 1 examines a view of inclusive caring in accordance with the views of Carol Gilligan (1982). Such a view of caring is premised on the idea of relationality – that is carer and cared-for are in a human relationship whereby they act in response to one another. Their responsiveness to one another prompts in them an understanding that caring manifests more appropriately in inclusive pedagogical encounters. In Chap. 2, I show how Nel Noddings's (1984) view on practical caring enhances pedagogical encounters. The idea of practical caring developed in this chapter is based on an understanding that caring is not aimless but rather oriented towards some practical purpose in which change is exercised. Practical caring is inextricably connected to an understanding that teachers and students can care only if their caring is directed towards addressing a particular situation or event that can be changed in a constructive and ethically responsible manner. Such a view of care is corroborated by Noddings, who considers care a matter of being reasonable within pedagogical relationships of mutuality and ethical action. Chapter 3 offers an account of authentic caring in reference to the seminal thoughts of Paulo Freire (2001) ably supported by the thoughts on critical pedagogy by Antonia Darder, Henry Giroux and Peter McLaren (with Jennifer Crawford and Nana Gyamfi, 2009). Following Freire, caring is authentic if it evokes critical understandings among teachers and students according to which they respond to particular pedagogical aspects. I specifically draw on Paulo Freire's (2001) ideas on care shown towards his students by accentuating what it means to care for and with them. Equally, I point out that teachers ought to act authentically to evoke the potentialities of their students as they open up students' minds to practice authentic and responsible care in society. The point is, in a Freirean way, care is extended beyond pedagogical encounters towards the cultivation of societal change. Chapter 4 elucidates a view of transactional or pragmatic caring as espoused through the work of Maurice Hamington (with Dorothy Miller, 2006). Transactional caring acknowledges that teachers and students are in some form of dialogue in terms of which both deliberate about matters that have societal implications. Quite pertinently, transactional caring as an instance of an ethic of care is in fact presented as a practice of socialising care. Thus, in a somewhat neo-Freirean way, care is extended to altering dire real-life situations through an idea of socialising care. Chapter 5 discusses Selma Sevenhuijsen's (2018) notion of attentive caring. Being attentive to one another, teachers and students avoid being dismissive and insulated. Instead, they recognise that attentiveness requires of them to respond caringly towards one another. Attentive caring begins with the self, with a willingness to reflect on our own actions and reactions, with the aim to enhance our interactions with others. Without attentive care, the possibility that people will actually care, dissipates, and the same accounts for practices within pedagogical encounters. In Chap. 6, I offer an exposition of democratic caring as articulated through the thoughts of Joan Tronto (2013). The view of democratic caring is commensurable with the notion of caring *with* others, which is distinctly different from caring about and caring for others within pedagogical encounters. For the first time in the book, I make a move distinctly away from caring *for* and caring *about* others towards caring *with* others in relation to Tronto's political idea of democratic caring. In a different way, democratic caring brings into prominence the idea that educational and/or pedagogical encounters have a political dimension without which education – and pedagogy for that matter – would fail to exist.

Chapter 7 offers an account of empathic caring as espoused through the seminal thoughts of Michael Slote (2007). Quite contentiously, Slote connects the ideas of empathy and caring in a way that ethicists like Tronto would be strictly opposed to. This chapter accentuates a move away from the separability of virtues such as empathy and caring and, envisages to combine the two concepts as Slote does. I argue that empathic caring is commensurate with an enactment of respect, dignity and justice towards people. Yet, I also show why and how empathic caring can be considered an extension of the notion of care with others. In Chap. 8, I draw on thoughts I have developed elsewhere to justify a notion of rhythmic caring (Davids & Waghid, 2017). Inasmuch as moments of attachment surface in pedagogical encounters, at the same time there also arise moments of detachment on account of scepticism. In other words, care as an act of rhythm is espoused as an act of advancing forward without inhibiting others from coming to speech. Simultaneously, in one's attempt to curb one's over-exuberance to care, you hold back on what you have to say in order that others' reasonable judgements can be strengthened without necessarily always having to rely on being taught. As an extension of my thoughts on ethical caring, in Chap. 9, I draw on David T. Hansen's (2011) views on cosmopolitanism to articulate a view of cosmopolitan caring. As in the case of empathic caring, I offer an account of cosmopolitan caring as an extension of ethical caring to show that caring in itself remains associated with other humane virtues such as cosmopolitanism and empathy. Chapter 10 examines a notion of *ubuntu* caring, and I show why and how African teaching and learning, in reference to a previous work done on a massive open online course (MOOC) (Waghid, Waghid, & Waghid, 2018), can be considered pedagogical encounters that ought to be deeply caring relations among teachers and students. In cultivating *ubuntu* caring, the possibility should always be there to change undesirable societal conditions. The point about *ubuntu* caring as an extension of ethical caring, is to show that caring can be associated with pedagogical encounters in African educational institutions, and that pedagogical relations in Africa are not unrelated to an ethic of care. Instead, pedagogical encounters are situationally enhanced through the cultivation of an ethic of *ubuntu* caring. In Chap. 11, I offer a reflective account of caring vis-à-vis my work as a journal editor and supervisor of doctoral students in a university setting. I specifically show how multiple dimensions of caring – as have been justified throughout this book – had a significant bearing on me, as editor, supervisor and dean of a faculty of education. I specifically highlight the notion of rhythmic caring in relation to dissonant pedagogical actions, such as discomfort, practical criticism and scepticism. More specifically, I elucidate why an ethic of care is an embodied pedagogical encounter, i.e. why academic inquiry is both inspired by reason and affect. Chapter 12 focuses on a philosophy of higher education in Africa influenced by a notion of rhythmic care. In this chapter, I show why and how a notion of caring is constitutive of a defensible philosophy of higher education in Africa. Such a philosophy, I contend, ought to be constituted by the notion of embodied and unconditional actions that have a strong link with compassion as an extension of an ethic of care. Chapter 13 addresses the notion of internal exclusion of women at African higher education institutions (HEIs). Together with Rachel Ndinelao Shanyanana, it is argued that women on the African continent experience moments of internal exclusion in HEIs that can be addressed through a notion of compassionate caring. In a coda, Chap. 14, entitled 'Educational technology, pedagogy and caring and espouses a notion of caring within online pedagogical encounters', Faiq Waghid and Zayd Waghid espouse a notion of technological caring – an instance of rhythmic caring within dissonance – in reference to their work with online students. The intention of this chapter is to show why caring within online pedagogical environments remains significant to any form of enhanced teaching and learning.

As a person working in philosophy of education for more than two decades, I have mostly researched notions of democratic citizenship education and how the underlying ideas of such theories influenced understandings of an African university and pedagogical encounters in (South) African universities. A central theme that emerged through my enunciations on what constitutes democratic citizenship education has been that of recognising oneself in relation to others and their otherness. Moreover, the most significant virtue that was always implicitly stated is the idea of being responsive to oneself and others. Hence, my attraction to an ethic of care on account of such an ethic seems to be in harmony with human relational commitments. However, my interest in care epistemology did not begin here.

A story, which affected my professional career as a scholar, three decades ago, when I was registered as a master's student at a local university, is appropriate here. One of my teachers evaluated one of my assignments about democratic educational theory. His most discouraging evaluative comment at the time related to my 'misunderstanding' of and 'muddled' writing about democratic educational theory. It is not the evaluative score that dismayed me most, but rather, that my attempt at producing a thoughtful piece of work was unduly dismissed. At that moment, I thought my university teacher was quite ruthless. After having given his 'harsh' treatment of my work some critical reflection, I thought about nothing else but faulting myself incessantly for not producing a credible piece of work. Rather than having resented my teacher, I silently thanked him for having pointed out a major deficiency in my articulation: incoherent and unclear expressions.

Even today, I often think about how that moment actually changed me as a scholar. As a result, I am always trying to write clearly, be coherent, and avoid being pedantic at all costs. This is the first time I offer my gratitude in writing to my philosophy of education teacher who passed away some five years ago: thank you for caring and for creating conditions for me to experience care! I thought my teacher was quite provocative at the time. However, it was his provocation that evoked a potentiality in me to improve my articulations. Nowadays, in my supervision of my own students, I use a soft touch of provocation in order to evoke the potentialities of my students to come to speech in their writing. As a recognition of my care, I will always feel intrinsically satisfied when I read my students' work and notice how lucidity and coherence dominate their writings in much the same way as my teacher wanted me to articulate myself so many years ago. It is this profound moment of care – when my potentiality was evoked to come to speech – that encouraged me to write this book. Thank you, Professor Wally Morrow, for instilling in me an ethic of care that has touched me forever in my academic relations with students and colleagues! I remain indebted to you for having shown much care during my years as a student in the faculty of education at the University of the Western Cape.

Subsequently, I have also pursued doctoral research under Professors Johann Steyn and Anton van Niekerk. My second PhD, with Professor Steyn, initiated me into thinking more lucidly about the notions of democracy and education, to the extent that I became increasingly attracted to aspects of social democratic theory. And, constitutive of what it means to enact socially, is the idea that people engage collectively within a spirit of attentiveness and care. Likewise, my third PhD brought me into relationship with the philosophy department at one of Africa's most prestigious universities. It was here that my encounters with Professor Van Niekerk brought me into conversation, for the first time, with deliberative democracy – a concept around which my understanding of community and care was built. Hence, throughout my doctoral encounters, I was provoked to think differently about democratic theory and practice. What I did not realise at the time, was that these doctoral encounters laid the foundation for my understanding of care both in relation to my supervisors and concomitant understandings of democratic education that ensued. In the same manner as above, I express my gratitude to my supervisors at Stellenbosch University who further stimulated my thinking in and about care in relation to education.

Cape Town, South Africa   Yusef Waghid

References

Agamben, G. (1994). *The man without content* (G. Albert, Trans.). Stanford, CA: Stanford University Press.
Braidotti, R. (2006). *Transpositions: On nomadic ethics*. Cambridge, UK: Polity Press.
Davids, N., & Waghid, Y. (2017). *Tolerance and dissent within education*. New York: Palgrave Macmillan.
Freire, P. (2001). *Pedagogy of freedom: Ethics, democracy, and civic courage*. Lanham, MD/Boulder, CO/New York/Oxford, UK: Rowman & Littlefield Publishers.
Gilligan, C. (1982). *In a different voice: Psychological theory and women's development*. Harvard, MA: Harvard University Press.
Hamington, M., & Miller, D. (Eds.). (2006). *Socializing care: Feminist ethics and public issues*. Oxford, UK: Rowman & Littlefield Publishers.
Hansen, D. T. (2011). *The teacher and the world: A study of cosmopolitanism as education*. London: Routledge.
Hedge, N., & Mackenzie, A. (2012). Beyond care? *Journal of Philosophy of Education, 46*(2), 192–206.
Noddings, N. (1984). *Caring: A feminine approach to ethics and moral education*. Berkeley, CA: University of California Press.
Noddings, N. (2006). *The challenge to care in schools: An alternative approach in education* (2nd ed.). New York: Teachers College/Columbia Press.
Nussbaum, M. (1997). *Cultivating humanity: A classical defence of reform in liberal education*. Cambridge, MA: Harvard University Press.
Rancière, J. (1991). *The ignorant schoolmaster: Five lessons in intellectual emancipation* (K. Ross, Trans.). Stanford, CA: Stanford University Press.
Sevenhuijsen, S. (2018). Care and attention. *South African Journal of Higher Education, 32*(6), 1–14.

Slote, M. (2007). *The ethics of care and empathy*. New York: Routledge.
Taylor, C. (1985). *Philosophy and the human sciences: Philosophical paper 2*. Cambridge, UK: Cambridge University Press.
Thompson, J. (2015). Towards an aesthetics of care. *The Journal of Applied Theatre and Performance, 20*(4), 430–441.
Tronto, J. (2013). *Caring democracy: Markets, equality and justice*. New York: New York University Press.
Waghid, Y. (1992). *Objective teacher evaluation and democracy in a changing South Africa*. Unpublished MA thesis, University of the Western Cape, Bellville, South Africa.
Waghid, Y. (1995). *Are problems in South African madaris due to an inadequate concept of madrassah schooling?* Unpublished PhD thesis, University of the Western Cape, Bellville, South Africa.
Waghid, Y. (2000). *Democratic education and praxis within higher education*. Unpublished PhD thesis, Stellenbosch University, Stellenbosch, South Africa.
Waghid, Y. (2001). *Democracy and community in South Africa: Liberal versus communitarian perspectives*. Unpublished PhD thesis, Stellenbosch University, Stellenbosch, South Africa.
Waghid, Y., Waghid, F., & Waghid, Z. (2018). *Rupturing African teaching and learning: Ubuntu justice and education*. New York: Palgrave Macmillan.

Acknowledgement

Chapter 13 is an amended version of an article published in the *South African Journal of Higher Education,* Volume 28 Number 4 in 2014. Permission was granted.

I thank my institution, Stellenbosch University, for granting me a research opportunity during 2018 to complete this project. I am also grateful to the Vice-Rector: Research, Professor Eugene Cloete, for supporting the editing of the book financially.

I remain indebted to Eleanor Christie and Rebecca Wyde of Palgrave Macmillan for their continuous support in making this manuscript reach fruition.

Contents

1 Caring and Democratic Inclusion 1

2 Cultivating Practical Caring 13

3 Authentic Caring: The Quest for Authoritative Teaching and Autonomous Learning 25

4 Transactional or Pragmatic Caring: Enacting Care-Giving and Care Receiving 39

5 Attentive Caring: On Coming into Presence Within Pedagogical Encounters 49

6 Democratic Caring: Building Relations of Freedom, Equality and Emancipation 55

7 Empathic Caring 63

8	Towards Rhythmic Caring: Cultivating Sceptical Pedagogical Encounters	71
9	Cosmopolitan Caring: On Reflexive Loyalty to the Known and Reflexive Openness to the New	81
10	*Ubuntu* Caring: Cultivating Moral, Compassionate, and Restorative Justice in University Education	89
11	A Reflective Account on Dimensions of Caring: Moments of Care Within Journal Editorship, Doctoral Supervision, and Deanship	97
12	Cultivating Care: Towards a Philosophy of Higher Education in Africa	113
13	Towards a Re-imagined Notion of University Education: In Defence of a Reconstituted Ethics of Care	129
14	Coda: Educational Technology, Pedagogy and Caring	159
Index		173

About the Author

Yusef Waghid is currently Distinguished Professor of Philosophy of Education in the Department of Education Policy Studies at Stellenbosch University. He is editor-in-chief of the *South African Journal of Higher Education,* and principal editor of the internationally acclaimed journal, *Citizenship Teaching and Learning*. His latest books, include *Teaching and Learning as a Pedagogic Pilgrimage: Cultivating Faith, Hope and Wonder* (London: Routledge, with Nuraan Davids, 2018) and *Rupturing African Philosophy of Teaching and Learning* (New York & London: Palgrave Macmillan, with Faiq Waghid & Zayd Waghid, 2018).

1

Caring and Democratic Inclusion

Introduction

Practices of university teaching and learning have long been associated with interrelated human experiences. A teacher teaches, and students learn. However, over the last three decades, since the post-critical turn, teaching and learning have been considered as interrelated human actions in the sense that, as a teacher performs the act of teaching, so he or she equally learns. Similarly, as students learn what they are taught, so they too become inclined towards teaching. In other words, it is not simply a matter of a teacher performing an act of teaching, and alternatively, a student learning. Rather, both teaching and learning have become intertwined activities in the sense that teaching–learning exists together. For purposes of this book, I refer to such an interrelationship of teaching–learning, a pedagogical encounter. By implication, pedagogical encounters constitute interrelated and inclusive human experiences of teaching and learning.

My contention is that pedagogical encounters among university teachers and students can be more inclusive if enacted upon through a notion of caring whose primary aim is to get participants (students and teachers) engaging evocatively. When students and teachers are evoked within pedagogical encounters, the possibility is always there for them to be aroused by one another's understandings and rational judgements. Put differently, when teachers teach, the possibility is always there for students to learn, thus, opening them up to understandings of what they have been taught. Students' potentialities are evoked if they make sense of their learning in one way or another. I want to suggest here that something else, in addition to teaching and learning, ought to take place to make pedagogical encounters more inclusive. Based on my own experiences in higher education and my readings on the matter, I am persuaded that the virtue of caring is a way in which pedagogical encounters can be enhanced. In this chapter, in reference to Carol Gilligan's work, I endeavour to give an account of what it means to evoke the potentialities of students and teachers with the aim to show how caring manifests in pedagogical – mostly teaching and learning – encounters, in particular focusing on how such encounters can become more inclusive.

An Ethic of Care as an Act of Inclusion

When Carol Gilligan (1982) produced her international bestseller, *In a different voice,* which she began writing in the early 1970s at a time of resurgence in feminist studies, it seemed obvious to her that as a psychologist 'differences in the body, in family relationships, and in societal and cultural position would make a difference psychologically' (Gilligan, 1982: xi). Little did she know at the time that her contribution to feminist scholarship would revolutionise and inspire educational research. Of interest to me, is her position on an ethic of care that is highlighted on occasions in her book, and its implications for pedagogical encounters.

In the main, her argument focuses on women's sense of integrity, which she contends is intertwined with an ethic of care. Women's integrity becomes manifest when they see themselves as women in 'a relationship of connection' with others, such as children, men and other women (Gilligan, 1982: 171). In other words, for Gilligan, an ethic of care is constituted in human interrelationships based on an authenticity of inclusion. I am reminded of an event that sparked my own entrance into academic life. Professor Shirley Pendlebury, who happened to be one of the examiners of my PhD, arranged that I present my first ever academic paper at the International Network of Philosophers of Education (INPE) Biennial Conference held in Johannesburg in August 1996. She was extremely caring in the sense that she offered me accommodation in her home in Melville for the duration of the conference. I slept in her personal library. Not only did I have the opportunity to browse through some of her books, but the conference attendance also initiated my professional career in the international community of philosophers of education. I subsequently attended INPE conferences in Sydney (2000), Oslo (2002), Madrid (2004), Malta (2006), Kyoto (2008), Addis Ababa (2012, as one of the guest speakers to co-deliver the Terrence McLaughlin Memorial Lecture), Cosenza (2016), only having missed Ankara (2010) and Bogota (2014). I am extremely grateful to Shirley and later Professor Paul Smeyers who included me through their care into the works of the INPE in which I eventually served as executive member between 2012 and 2018. Ever since, I remained in a relational connection with the organisation that advances global academic interests in philosophy of education.

Now, when a genuine relationship of inclusiveness is cultivated by men and women, such a relationship rests on 'the premise of nonviolence' (Gilligan, 1982: 174). Simply put, an ethic of care manifests in human relationships and is constituted by nonviolence. Personally and professionally, I was never affronted within the INPE, except on one occasion when a presentation in Madrid (2004) was rendered in opposition to the idea of an African philosophy of education. As an African, I felt somewhat let down because fellow South Africans deemed it important to take issue with a notion of philosophy of education, which they considered antithetical to any plausible notion of the concept. For Penny Enslin and Kai Horsthemke, an indigenous African philosophy of education, particularly the notion of *ubuntu* (humanness and human interdependence) did not have the academic feasibility to warrant an existence as a defensible philosophy of education. Of course, I disagreed. Until recently, when I encountered Penny again at the Philosophy of Education Society of Great Britain (PESGB) conference in Oxford in 2018, she softly asked me whether I still had a problem with her (Penny's) criticism of African philosophy of education. In a caringly inclusive manner – as Gilligan would assert – I said that any philosophy of education – including an African one for that matter – ought to be subjected to criticism if it warrants an existence as a philosophy of education. It is not so much my encounter with Penny at the breakfast table that reminds me of our ongoing friendship in academe, but more profoundly the practice of inclusive caring that seemed to have informed our relationship as peers for many years. Indeed, an ethic of inclusive care always characterise my professional relations with academic friends – a relationship of nonviolence where friends co-exist in an atmosphere of mutual criticism as espoused by Gilligan.

At least, three aspects emerge from Gilligan's understanding of an ethic of care: firstly, caring is a form of human attachment (Gilligan, 1982: 63) according to which humans do not act hurtfully towards others (Gilligan, 1982: 51). The latter implies that people cannot be silenced when they speak in their own voices – that is, they do not experience a violation and exclusion when they proffer a different point of view. Penny and Kai proffered a different understanding of an African philosophy of education. Yet, we have not been detached from one another's work. We remain attached within the encounter without harming, ridiculing or caricaturing one another. Doing so, would not only undermine an ethic of care, but also open up the possibility of excluding one another from and within encounters. Although, at a crucial time during South Africa's post-apartheid years in the mid-1990s to mid-2000s, emerging black academics vociferously considered an alignment with genuine African scholarship as a way to express their allegiance to a transformative democratic agenda. Any attempt that seemed to have jeopardised the aspiration of black scholarship for a legitimate philosophy of African education, was considered unjust and contrary to the transformation of the higher education (HE) agenda. With this background in mind, I witnessed glaring disagreements among scholars who defended the notion of an African philosophy of education, and those who opposed such a view. It is within such a context that my own defence of an African philosophy of education gained more support among black scholarship, and rivalled positions were conceived as antidemocratic and even racist, to say the least. In this regard, a prominent journal in South Africa, *Journal of Education* managed by the Kenton

Association of South Africa, deemed it important to publish a series of articles that dealt with an advancement of African philosophy of education in 2004/2005. Most notably, my own initial views on a defence of African philosophy of education were published in the same journal in which I began to connect the cultivation of such a philosophy of education with the democratisation of education in Africa (Waghid, 2004). In a different way, my initial defence of an African philosophy of education can be considered an act of inclusive caring as I endeavoured to engage with others about the feasibility or not of such a discourse in a professional and public manner.

The afore-mentioned discussions on what constitutes an African philosophy of education also informed deliberations among students and myself. Heated debates often ensued without students and myself ever leaving the deliberations. Not surprisingly, the students and I produced a book, entitled *African(a) philosophy of education: (Re)constructions and deconstructions* (Waghid & Van Wyk, 2005), in which some of the leading debates on the concept of an African philosophy of education were collected as an anthology of essays. The point about this book was to show how people with different views on an African philosophy of education can deliberate yet remain present within the encounter. Pedagogically speaking, teachers do not care for students when they insult or deride the students. Teachers care for students when they (i.e. the teachers) are attentive to the different voices of students, and thus ensure that the students remain included in pedagogical encounters. Any form of exclusion is tantamount to perpetrating violence against the excluded, and violence occurs only when human encounters are ruptured by derision and disrespect – that is, when caring is wanting. When, teachers act dismissively towards students as if the latter do not have anything meaningful to contribute to pedagogical encounters, then one can claim that caring is absent. Equally, when students do not pay much attention to teachers' explanations about this or that matter, then caring is also absent for the reason that humans ought to be engaged inclusively for caring to have any effect on human encounters. The point is, caring is an act of inter-relationality and any attempt at excluding the other undermines the notion of care. As cogently stated by Gilligan (1982: 63), an ethic of care is an ideal human relationship:

> [T]he vision that self and other will be treated as of equal worth, that despite differences in power, things will be fair; the vision that everyone will be responded to and included, that no one will be left alone and hurt.

Secondly, an ethic of care is a relational act. Quite poignantly, Gilligan (1982: xvi) relates such relationality to being human and a speaking being. In her words, 'to have a voice is to be human. To have something to say is to be a person. But speaking depends on listening and being heard; it is an intentionally relational act'. An ethic of care is exercised when someone speaks and another person listens. One cannot assume to care without being in communication with someone else. A university teacher cannot be said to care for students if he or she shows no interest in communicating with them – that is, making them understand his or her speech acts. Students cannot be said to be cared for if they are not placed in a position of listening to the speech of a teacher. In a way, caring manifests when the relationship between a teacher and a student evolves into one of speaking and listening. That is to say, when a teacher speaks without the possibility of students listening to him or her, it would be difficult to say that the relationship between them is constituted by caring. Thus, caring does not happen only when a teacher speaks. However, when such a teacher's speech is being listened to together with his or her speaking, caring is enacted. This implies that students have to consider what a teacher has to say and then make sense of his or her speech before it can be claimed that they are listening to the teacher and, by implication, that the teacher cares.

It might be that students show their disinterest in what a teacher has to say or, alternatively, it might also be that students are not satisfied with what they listen to. Showing dissatisfaction and disinterest towards speech does not mean that such speech is not listened to. The very act of students' displeasure towards a teacher's speech is not a justification for dismissing the act of relationality between a teacher and students. The mere fact that students are annoyed with a teacher's speech means that their discontent is a consequence of having made sense of speech or not. The point is that disagreement between a teacher and students does not nullify their relationality. Caring can still be present although disagreement is at play. In fact, caring can also flourish through dissensus or agreement. When dissensus occurs, neither the teacher nor the students are in agreement with what is being listened to or spoken, respectively. Disagreement means that someone talks back to what is being heard and, in this way, brings what is being heard into controversy. In turn, speakers are provoked to come up with more tenable speech that could possibly convince those listening to it. Disagreement seems to enhance relationality and by implication enlarges caring. As Gilligan (1982: 48, author's own emphases) herself notes, '... "Caring" traces a path which remains largely unexplored, a narrative of deprivation followed by *enhancement* in which *connection*, though leading through separation, is in the end maintained or restored.'

Thirdly, an ethic of care is open to enacting one's responsibility towards oneself and others. The connection between an ethic of care and human responsibility is explained as the ability of people to speak their minds without having to face aggressive behaviour towards them (Gilligan, 1982: 173). Of course, the absence of hostility does not imply that engaging relationships among people should not be belligerent or distressful. Belligerence and distress within pedagogical relations cannot be equated with hostility. According to Eamonn Callan (1997: 210), pedagogical encounters often involve ethical confrontations that should be characterised by 'a certain belligerence [conditioned by] the avoidance of outright verbal abuse'. In other words, any 'productive confrontation' of an ethical kind is sometimes needed in order for participants – say, teachers and students – to be prepared to deal with their passions and 'morally distracting emotions that confrontation is liable to release' (Callan, 1997: 211). Belligerent and distressful behaviour 'may disturb doubts about the correctness of our moral beliefs or about the importance of the differences between what we and others believe' (Callan, 1997: 212). Through inserting doubts belligerently and distressfully into pedagogical encounters, the possibility of combat 'must give way eventually to moments of ethical conciliation when the truth and error in rival positions has been made clear, and a fitting synthesis of factional viewpoints is achieved' (Callan, 1997: 212). In this way, teachers and students would exercise their responsibility towards one another – that is, they would treat one another with care because the ethical confrontation has never spilled over into a verbal enmity among teachers and students. It is the task of an ethic of care to provoke teachers and students 'to think wisely about the difference between reasonable and unreasonable pluralism, and as far as unreasonable pluralism is a part of our lives, there is much that we cannot agree to disagree about' (Callan, 1997: 215). Even disagreeing belligerently and distressfully should not close the door to remaining open-minded to a plurality of opinions and controversial issues. Acting with care and by implication, responsibility, should always keep teachers and students open to the possibility that pedagogical encounters can at times be quite belligerent and distressful. However, except for verbal intimidation, belligerent and distressful pedagogical encounters should be about raising doubts within the understandings of teachers and students. As aptly, remarked by Callan (1997: 222), a pedagogical encounter –

> [T]hat honours the distinction between reasonable and unreasonable pluralism will not be the sedate and harmonious endeavor we might sometimes want it to be. The many different conceptions of value that we bring to deliberation will generate moral friction and distress, and if the virtues of reasonable citizenship can often contain the friction and distress, the latter may also work to block the development of those virtues or erode them when they are already in place.

In sum, I argue that an ethic of care is conceptually linked to the practice of inclusion. According to the seminal thoughts of Carol Gilligan (1982), an ethic of care is constituted by at least three aspects of human action: the presence of non-aggressive human attachments; acts of relationality among people; and responsible human action of an ethical kind that invokes at times belligerence and distress. Next, I discuss the connection between an ethic of care and the notion of democratic inclusion.

Caring Constitutes Democratic Inclusion

Following Gilligan's (1982) understanding of an ethic of care, human attachment in relational fashion underscored by the capacity to act responsibly seems to guide her notion of caring. Of course, at the centre of such an ethic of care is the idea that human beings speak to and with one another separated from acts of hostility. When humans speak, they 'make proposals and criticize one another, and aim to persuade one another of the best solution to collective problems' (Young, 2000: 52). It is such a communicative activity of speaking that connects with reasonableness, openness and accountability to others, as Young (2000: 52) asserts. In other words, when humans speak with care, they remain attached to one another on the basis of a relational experience of openness whereby they hold one another responsible for their speech acts. When the latter occurs, they can be said to be engaged in a process of democratic inclusion. Penny Enslin and I have remained in communication irrespective of our contending views on an African philosophy of education. Young (2000: 52) makes the point that when humans as members of the polity are democratically included, they are 'included equally in the decision-making process and have an equal opportunity to influence the outcome'. What follows from the afore-mentioned, is that democratic action mandates inclusion because people 'must listen to others with differing positions to whom they are also answerable' (Young, 2000: 52). It is through inclusion that people can engage in deliberation, criticism and responsible actions. When the latter happens, people can be said to engage in caring relationships on the grounds that an ethic care invokes disagreement, human engagement (attachment), and responsibility towards one another's speech acts. Simply put, democratic inclusion makes possible the enactment of speaking and listening (deliberation), disagreement (that could also lead to dissensus), and responsibility towards others. In this way, democratic inclusion is conceptually related to an ethic of care.

In addition, as aptly identified by Young (2000: 53), democratic communication (inclusion) and, by implication, an ethic of care, would be seriously constrained by the exercise of external and internal exclusion. On the one hand, Young (2000: 54) avers that external exclusion involves ways in which individuals and groups that ought to be included are purposely and inadvertently left out of democratic encounters. For instance, some university students have a legitimate and equal right to engage in a pedagogical encounter. Yet, on account of these students having to participate in, say, an event organised simultaneously by student administration, they would be unable to participate a learning experience and thus not be in a position to influence decisions taken during the pedagogical encounter. They are kept out of the encounter and are externally excluded from deliberations in and about pedagogical matters. On the other hand, although students are formally included in a pedagogical encounter, they may find that their views and claims are not taken equally into account. They might experience moments of not having something worthy of consideration to say – that is, they might experience moments of not being treated with equal respect, say by university teachers. Young (2000: 55) refers to such experiences as being subjected to 'internal exclusion, because they concern ways that people [students] lack effective opportunity to influence the thinking of others even when they have access to [such pedagogical encounters]'. As a consequence of the possibility of both external and internal exclusion, Young (2000: 56) contends the following:

> A theory of democratic inclusion [that resonates with an ethic of care] requires an expanded conception of political communication, both in order to identify modes of internal inclusion and to provide and account of more inclusive possibilities of attending to one another in order to reach understanding.

It is democratic inclusion and its concomitant link to an ethic of care that can produce equal respect and trust among participants, in this case, teachers and students. Likewise, democratic inclusion can also make possible understanding across structural and cultural differences, and motivate recognition of one another through communicative action (Young, 2000: 57). Once again, as Young (2000: 61) cogently posits, recognition on account of democratic inclusion and an ethic of care for that matter, is primarily a starting point for political and pedagogic engagement and contestation – that is, actions that hold human relationality in high esteem, and which Gilligan (1982: 139) equates with the fulfilment of a responsibility to care for others. And, rather than excluding others (students) from pedagogical encounters and abandoning their feelings of care, teachers who endeavour to care for students act responsibly by making every effort not only to connect with students but also to sustain their pedagogical encounters through acts of care (Gilligan, 1982: 127).

Summary

In this chapter, I considered Carol Gilligan's (1982) groundbreaking account of caring in relation to an ethic of care that invokes the ideas of human attachment (inclusion), relationality (interconnectedness) and responsibility. At the core of democratic human action is an ethic of care that engenders human interrelationships, which are commensurate with speech acts that are reasonable, responsive to difference, and inclined to moments of belligerence and distress within pedagogical encounters. If such an ethic of care prevails, there is always the possibility that human relations will be swayed towards mutual respect and trust, the recognition of difference and disagreement, and a genuine endeavour to act responsibly toward all participants within pedagogical encounters. At the heart of the afore-mentioned democratically inspired actions is the idea that humans ought to speak their minds and be listened to. Without the courage of speaking and listening to others, human beings will not be in relation to one another and, they will not exercise their equal opportunity to act with responsibility towards themselves and others. In brief, caring will remain an act of inclusion as long as democratic aspirations of speaking and listening are respectfully and humanely enacted. Only then the possibility exists that humans' acts of responsibility will be enhanced. Such a notion of caring foregrounds the possibility that pedagogical encounters can be mutually engaging, respectful and oriented towards human responsibility, if encounters are constituted by inclusive care. And, if care manifests, the possibility of mutual trust will prevail whereby teachers and students would be prepared to remain participants within such democratically inclusive encounters. In the next chapter, the afore-mentioned elucidation of inclusive caring will be extended to what Nell Noddings (1984) refers to as practical caring.

References

Callan, E. (1997). *Creating citizens: Political education and liberal democracy.* Oxford, UK: Oxford University Press.
Gilligan, C. (1982). *In a different voice: Psychological theory and women's development.* Cambridge, MA: Harvard University Press.

Noddings, N. (1984). *Caring: A feminine approach to ethics and moral education*. Berkeley, CA: University of California Press.

Waghid, Y. (2004). Revisiting the African-Africana philosophy of education debate: Implications for university teaching. *Journal of Education, 34*, 127–142.

Waghid, Y., & Van Wyk, B. (Eds.). (2005). *African(a) philosophy of education: (Re)constructions and deconstructions*. Stellenbosch, South Africa: African Sun Press.

Young, I. M. (2000). *Inclusion and democracy*. Oxford, UK: Oxford University Press.

2

Cultivating Practical Caring

Introduction

The concept 'practical caring' intimates two interrelated ideas: caring and practicality. Of course, one can argue that caring in itself is some kind of doing action and therefore does not require any affirmation of its practical nature, as doing implies some sort of practical action. However, to accentuate the nature of the particular type of caring discussed in this chapter, it seems apposite to refer to the concept of 'practical caring'. The point about such a kind of caring is that the effects of caring in this manner has some relation to the effects it engenders. In Nel Noddings's (1984) seminal work, *Caring: A feminine approach to ethics and moral education*, she describes the concept 'caring' as a state of consciousness of a carer constituted by engrossment (an open receptivity) and motivational displacement or concern towards the cared-for. Extending the latter view, and in recognition of Carol Gilligan's (1982) notion of inclusive caring, Noddings (1992: 21) posits that, in addition to caring being reasonable in the sense that it emphasises an individual attribute of a carer, it also recognises the mutual part played by the cared-for in 'an ethic of relation'. Put differently, caring –

© The Author(s) 2019
Y. Waghid, *Towards a Philosophy of Caring in Higher Education*,
https://doi.org/10.1007/978-3-030-03961-5_2

[H]as its own rationality or reasonableness, and in appropriate situations carers draw freely on standard linear rationality as well. But its emphasis is on living together, on creating, maintaining, and enhancing positive relations – not on decision-making in moments of high moral conflict, nor on justification. (Noddings, 1992: 21)

Considering that caring is an act of relationality, I shall now, with reference to Noddings's ideas, look at three practices that cultivate caring, namely modelling (showing), dialogue and confirmation (recognition).

Modelling (Showing), Dialogue and Confirmation as Constitutive of Caring

Noddings connects her explication of caring to a discourse of moral education that is constituted by modelling (showing), dialogue and confirmation (recognition) – all constitutive aspects of what can be referred to as practical caring (Noddings, 1984). Unlike Noddings, I do not consider practice as another separate feature of caring for the reason that caring is a doing action that implies performing a practice. Likewise, modelling, dialogue and confirmation are practices within themselves. Firstly, for Noddings (1992: 22, my emphases), it is not sufficient to '*tell* our students to care; we *show* them how to care by, creating caring relations with them'. In other words, caring has to be modelled or showed. For example, a university teacher does not merely inform students about concepts and practices in philosophy of education, such as arguments and argumentation. Rather, a university teacher cares for students when he or she shows them what arguments entail, and how to construct arguments. In this regard, showing students the rigour of arguments and argumentation, Noddings (1992: 172) accentuates the following:

> They [students] should be introduced to the full rigor and beauty of the disciplines of the study [that is, arguments]. Hard questions should be asked, and epistemologically excellent responses should be expected.

Likewise, when a student does not yet understand argumentation, it seems more appropriate for him or her (i.e. the student) to learn 'to be a responsive cared-for' individual (Noddings, 1992: 22). When university students (the cared-for) are initiated into a discourse of argumentation, it would be prudent to appreciate the rigour of argumentation on the part of students, modelled (i.e. shown) by a teacher (carer) in order to cultivate the caring relationship. Modelling (or showing), as an instance of practical caring, is not aimed at producing unquestioning students who merely learn what it means to proffer arguments. Rather, modelling is a pedagogic act of teaching that can invite students (the cared-for) to bring into question what their carers (university teachers) have to say, and then to articulate more informed and alternative understandings. The point I am making, is that caring for students through modelling is not a way of coercing students to learn. Instead, modelling is a pedagogic opportunity for both teaching and learning undergirded by an ethic of caring — that is, through modelling teachers *show* students how to construct, reconstruct and perhaps deconstruct arguments in a philosophy class. Simultaneously, students learn to appreciate argumentation with the intent to enact their autonomous ways of proposing their own arguments. Of course, the emphasis in pedagogic relationships is not on modelling, but rather on how caring manifests. In addition, modelling is a way by which carers can initiate the cared-for into a discourse of learning through care. In this way, practical caring can possibly be shown (modelled) and become manifest in pedagogic encounters among teachers and students.

Of course, my potential critic might claim that modelling as an instance of caring is a dogmatic pedagogic approach on the grounds that students learn in relation to what they see through a teacher's example. In a different way, through modelling, my critic might assert, students are coerced to follow a teacher's example and thus have no space to become their own selves. In an attempt to challenge such a criticism of Noddings's notion of modelling, I draw on the thoughts of Peters, Burbules, and Smeyers (2008) who explain an aspect of the philosopher, Ludwig Wittgenstein's pedagogy of teaching and learning. In their book, *Showing and doing: Wittgenstein as a pedagogical philosopher*, they present a plausible argument to defend a reread of Wittgenstein's (1922) *Tractatus Logico-Philosophicus* from the perspective of philosophy of education. Their argument is that one has to read the *Tractatus* 'at the level of what it *says* and at the level of what it *shows*' (Peters et al., 2008: 67). Of interest to me, is their claim that the *Tractatus*, which is full of metaphors, thought-experiments, examples and puzzles, represents a teaching (and learning I would assert) approach written in a pictorial theory of language according to which not everything is said in writing. In a way, the *Tractatus* expresses incomplete truths about the world and the reader has to catch up somewhat with what has not been made entirely explicit. The text of the *Tractatus* 'remain[s] mired in the domain of facts, without creating an opportunity for students to reflect on how they came to be *facts* … [it] only creates the conditions of a possibility' (Peters et al., 2008: 77–78). My understanding of such a view is that Wittgenstein's picture theory seems to suggest that learning is possible without students having to be told everything they need to know. Instead, like modelling, some things cannot be made entirely clear to students because '[c]larity is a *learned* outcome, something achieved, not something that can be directly provided to another' (Peters et al., 2008: 80). Students should therefore use the possibility to see things for themselves on the grounds that they are not told everything, including constructing alternative understandings based on what they themselves have come to see. And, when students come to see particular ways of looking at the world, there is always the possibility that they may begin to see things differently for themselves. In this way, modelling or showing is not such a pernicious pedagogic approach to teaching and learning. Rather, modelling or showing emanates from the possibility of not having been told and provided everything by teachers. At times, not being told everything by teachers evokes understandings in students to search for meanings themselves. And, the more they think about meanings in the light of what they have not been informed about, alternative meanings come up – that is, *show* themselves as a consequence of deeper thinking and engagement with existing understandings. This way, students might also begin to see things that have not been there previously. That is, new, alternative meanings have shown themselves.

In relation to the above understanding of showing as an instance of caring, I specifically think of Professor Nic Burbules's visit to my institution some fifteen years ago. He taught master's students a lesson on the difference between discussion, conversation, debate and deliberation. He presented his arguments in such a convincing way that students were not provided with everything about what the afore-mentioned democratic acts entail. Instead, Burbules showed the students enough to have prompted them to develop their own independent understandings of democratic action. As a corollary of how students have been initiated into rudimentary understandings of democratic action, they eventually offered alternate understandings of such actions without the support always of the presenter. And, what students came to see was a consequence of having had to make up grounds in constructing their autonomous understandings of democratic action. After students had been shown how to construct, reconstruct and deconstruct arguments, they went on to produce their own independent understandings of what four different notions of democratic education entail. It was as if they had been exposed to a Tractarean pictorial theory (Wittgenstein, 1922) according to which they developed their autonomous views on democratic action.

Secondly, following Noddings (1992: 23), caring relations are most appropriately enhanced through dialogical action. This is so, on the basis that dialogue is open-ended, and the possibility that participants in the dialogue would be coerced to come to some sort of agreement is not necessarily a requirement. What is the point of engaging in dialogue with the aim to reach consensus if dialogue in itself, at least a form of dialogue commensurate with caring, ought to remain open-ended? In a caring relationship, humans are attentive to one another, and they do not necessarily engage in dialogue to achieve some sort of desired outcome. As aptly stated by Noddings (1992: 23),

> Dialogue serves another purpose in moral education. It connects us to each other and helps to maintain caring relations. It also provides us with the knowledge of each other that forms a foundation for response in caring … Dialogue is implied in the criterion of engrossment. To receive the other is to attend fully and openly. Continuing dialogue builds up a substantial knowledge of one another that serves to guide our responses.

Following on the above, dialogue (as a caring relationship) can result in both consensus and dissensus. The open-endedness of dialogue subjects it to both agreement and disagreement between the cared and the cared-for. It is not that individuals or groups engage in dialogue for the sole purpose of achieving a desired outcome. Rather, people engage in dialogue on account of connecting to one another, and if a particular outcome is achieved, it is as a consequence of people's attunement to engage with one another. Next, I want to examine such a caring dialogical relation further, vis-à-vis Jacques Rancière's notion of disagreement in and through human action.

According to Rancière (2016a: 83), if human encounters were to bear any fruit, then debate ought to identify its point of disagreement. In disagreement –

> Every situation can be cracked open on the inside, reconfigured in a different regime of perception and signification, altering the landscape of what can be seen and what can be thought, along with the field of the possible and the distribution of capacities and incapacities. (Rancière, 2016b: 155)

My understanding of situations being 'cracked open from the inside' has a link with the notion of disruption in the sense that when people disagree they are placed in a position, firstly, to see things as being otherwise or new; and secondly, to look at the possibility of reconfiguring their understandings of things. Put differently, disagreement allows individuals to alter or disrupt their understandings of thoughts and practices. According to Rancière (2016b: 146), disruption/alteration 'is the affirmation of their [the individuals'] capacity to reconstruct their world of experience, therefore to take their part in the global reconfiguration of the social world'.

But, for individuals to reconfigure their understandings of thoughts and social practices, they have to exercise their equality as 'speaking being[s]' (Rancière, 2016b: 151). When individuals act as equal speaking beings, they show their capacity to speak their minds and to contribute and alter conversations. In other words, they are not merely told what to think and say, instead, they are summoned to express their equal intelligence. And, when individuals exercise their capacity of equality in such a way, they are no longer dominated and exploited, but have developed the capacity to resist and reject assumptions about themselves and the situations in which they find themselves, what Rancière (2016b: 155) refers to as giving way to 'a multiplicity of forms and scenes of dissensus'. Put differently, individuals' exercising of equality lends itself to disagreement and by implication, alterations and unpredictable situations.

Pedagogically speaking, university teachers and students exercise their equality when they speak their minds. They make claims about the university texts to which they are exposed, make decisions to reconfigure ideas, look for alternative ways of understanding issues, and take the time to engage with one another's thoughts to the extent that they either agree or disagree. When teachers and students engage in such equal ways, they become emancipated as they are never coerced to stand by the decisions someone else proposed to them. They are engaged in what Rancière (2016b: 139) refers to as an 'intellectual adventure' on the basis that they participate in an 'intelligence of anybody' – that is, neither teachers nor students wait to be taught and they make time to go to pedagogically unforeseen places.

Thus, when university teachers and students engage in an 'intellectual adventure' they become prone to express their equal intelligence. They come to speech on the basis of having developed the capacity to see things for themselves and to make judgements about intellectual concerns. Their equality of speech is geared towards disruption and emancipation and for once they do not feel constrained that their readings of university texts would be thought of as ignorant. Instead, they affirm their capacities to alter understandings on the basis of their intellectual equality. As cogently stated by Rancière (2016b: 151):

> This is an exercise in the method of equality that draws the treatment of the philosopher, the verse of the poet, the narration of the historian, and the article of the worker out of their 'specific' territory and status and considers them as performances of speaking beings about what it means to be a speaking being.

When teachers and students act as speaking beings, they make their equality known to one another on the basis that they can alter their thinking and ways of seeing the world. Since teachers and students have equal capacity to enact change in the social world, they can challenge forces of domination, narcissism and rebellion – those aspects of human life that make emancipation of the self and others impossible (Rancière, 2016b: 154). Put differently, equal speaking beings have the capacities to bring about practical changes in the social world through disruption and reconfiguration of thought. In this way, their potential dissensus reached within and about social matters is an affirmation of their equal capacities to reconfigure the world. In short, they are as much equal beings as they are caring beings.

Thirdly, Noddings (1992: 25) links the practice of caring to the idea of confirmation, which implies 'an act of affirming and encouraging the best in others'. In her words,

> When we confirm someone, we spot a better self and encourage its development. We can do this only if we know the other well enough to see what he or she is trying to become. Formulas and slogans have no place here. We do not set up a single ideal or set of expectations for everyone to meet, but we identify something admirable, or at least acceptable, struggling to emerge in each person we encounter. The person working toward a better self must see the attribute or goal as worthy, and we too must see it as at least morally acceptable ... Confirmation lifts us toward our vision of a better self. (Noddings, 1992: 25)

Noddings's notion of caring as an act of confirmation reminds one of Rancière's (2016a: 84) elucidation of recognition. For him, recognition can mean two things:

> [First,] 'the coincidence of an actual perception with a knowledge we already possess, as when we recognize a place, a person, a situation, or an argument'. Second, from a moral point of view, recognition means that we respond to the claim of other individuals who demand that we treat them as autonomous entities or equal persons. (Rancière, 2016a: 84)

Whereas Noddings emphasises the notion of confirmation as a recognition of individuals' self-confidence, self-respect and self-esteem, my interest is in Rancière's idea of 'recognition as an act of confirmation' (Rancière,

2016a: 84), that is how people 'construct themselves to the extent that they construct, even through struggle, relations of confidence, respect, and esteem with other people'. In other words, recognition and, by implication confirmation, is not just present when someone else recognises or confirms another – as Noddings conceives of confirmation – rather, recognition is 'a theory of the community asserting that the existence of a common world is a matter of intersubjective relationships … of mutual recognition' (Rancière, 2016a: 86). Therefore, like caring, recognition (confirmation) is present in the act of community when individuals identify others as autonomous and capable of becoming other.

In pedagogical encounters, university teachers and students can equally assert and enact their capacities to see texts in more satisfying ways. And, when they (teachers and students) are commended by one another for their fulfilling achievements and courage displayed in coming up with other gratifying interpretations, their analyses are extolled by others in quite respectful ways. The point I am making is that such forms of confirmation where teachers and students are respectfully recognised for their gratifying textual interpretations and justifications, are commensurate with acts of caring. Caring manifests when teachers and students are equally recognised for their dynamic, enriched and credible ways in which textual work is completed. In this regard, I concur with Noddings (1992: 25) when she posits that confirmational caring only happens when pedagogical relations of trust among teachers and students emerge. When students and teachers engage with one another in an atmosphere of mutual trust, they act respectfully and admirably towards one another thereby confirming and recognising one another's satisfying achievements. In such a way, caring becomes a pedagogical possibility. Here, I specifically think of student supervision. Students are especially encouraged when supervisors confirm that their writing and arguments are on track. Such recognition is necessary in the sense that students invariably require pedagogical authentication when tackling the daunting task of completing a thesis. And, it would not be undesirable for students when they are confirmed in pedagogically positive ways. Of course, I am not suggesting that supervisors who make negative comments about students' writing do not recognise such students' work. In some instances, it can be that negative remarks about students' writing can actually encourage students to produce more credible pieces of writing. By implication un-authentication could also result in a semblance of confirmation when supervisors affirm that some students' writing requires urgent attention. The point is, confirmation is an act of care that can support pedagogical encounters to remain practically plausible – that is, students and teachers will be equally recognised as they endeavour to care for one another in and through pedagogic encounters.

Summary

Thus far, I have shown that caring is in fact an act of community whereby individuals (teachers and students) engage with one another in pedagogical encounters in which they are influenced by one another's understandings and justifications. Caring in communicative pedagogical encounters unfolds in at least three ways: through an enactment of modelling (showing), dialogical action, and the recognition (confirmation) of one another. In turn, such caring relationships engender opportunities for both teachers and students to look at things differently, to alter the meanings of situations, and to become altered others. In this way, change is always in becoming when practical caring is showed, dialogised and confirmed. Pedagogical encounters invariably remain authentic if underscored by practical acts of care such as showing, dialogue and confirmation or recognition. In the next chapter, I specifically discuss the seminal thoughts of Paulo Freire on authentic caring.

References

Gilligan, C. (1982). *In a different voice: Psychological theory and women's development*. Cambridge, MA: Harvard University Press.
Noddings, N. (1984). *Caring: A feminine approach to ethics and moral education*. Berkeley, CA: University of California Press.
Noddings, N. (1992). *The challenge to care in schools: An alternative approach to education*. New York: Teachers College Press.

Peters, M. A., Burbules, N. C., & Smeyers, P. (2008). *Showing and doing: Wittgenstein as pedagogical philosopher*. Boulder, CO: Paradigm.

Rancière, J. (2016a). Critical questions on the theory of recognition. In K. Genel & J. P. Deranty (Eds.), *Recognition or disagreement: A critical encounter on the politics of freedom, equality, and identity* (pp. 83–95). New York: Columbia University Press.

Rancière, J. (2016b). The method of equality: Politics and poetics. In K. Genel & J. P. Deranty (Eds.), *Recognition or disagreement: A critical encounter on the politics of freedom, equality, and identity* (pp. 133–155). New York: Columbia University Press.

Wittgenstein, L. (1922). *Tractatus Logico-philosophicus*. London, UK: Kegan Paul, Trench & Trubner.

3

Authentic Caring: The Quest for Authoritative Teaching and Autonomous Learning

Introduction

I begin this chapter with a brief reflective account of my experience with my rooster. Considering that the rooster crows at least twenty-five times in the morning, I was concerned that my neighbours would become annoyed despite the fact that I live in a rural residential area with large open space. I decided to take the rooster to a farm but after I managed to cage him, I could see in his eyes the look of anger and frustration for not being able to graze freely. I felt very sad and decided after a while to release him. I am deeply attached to the rooster since he was a chicken and I could not dare witness his departure. When he was caged for a while, the situation evoked feelings of sadness in me and I wanted only to care for him. I could see his vulnerability in his eyes and felt that I disappointed him when he was trying to get out of the cage and knocked his head several times against the chicken wire that consequently resulted in an injury to his head. Of course, I subsequently liaised with my neighbour who confirmed that the rooster was not a disturbance to the peace as they hardly heard him. This incident with the rooster, especially when I saw blood flowing from his head, not only evoked feelings of compassion in me particularly driven by my conscience and sense of duty towards vulnerable animals, it also brought to mind three aspects of caring that I will consider in the context of Paulo Freire's (2001) ideas on care shown towards his students: to care for students, teachers act authentically in a committed way to evoke the potentialities of their students; to care implies that teachers act with authority as they open up students to the challenges of life through questioning – a matter of stimulating students to act with autonomy; and, to care for students implies that teachers act with an ethical responsibility towards them.

Freire on Caring Towards Students

At the time of writing this book, the educational world was celebrating the Brazilian educationist and activist, Paulo Freire's fiftieth anniversary since the publication of his monumental work, *Pedagogy of the oppressed* (1970). Undoubtedly, Freire is one of the most influential educators and activists of the twentieth century and his work has been affirmed as thoughtful explorations of ethics, education and democracy by one of the world's leading thinkers in philosophy, theology and education, Maxine Greene (1995, cited in Freire, 2001). In this context, I remember a story, which a colleague of mine narrated about Freire's *Pedagogy of the oppressed.* Professor Gerhard Zecha from the University of Salzburg, Austria, briefly told me that when he first arrived in South Africa on invitation from one of the local universities in the 1980s, he was vigorously questioned at the airport on arrival. Custom officers also confiscated his copy of *Pedagogy of the oppressed,* considered at the time by the apartheid police and customs as an illegal book because it would conscientise students – quite bizarrely in a Freirean fashion – to undermine higher education in the country. Similarly, my own post-graduate education at a university of the left – University of the Western Cape – in the early 1990s, exposed me once again to the seminal writings of Paulo Freire, and his *Pedagogy of the oppressed* was used as a transformative text in the faculty where I studied. Any student in the Faculty of Education in the late 1980s and early 1990s invariably encountered this seminal text of Freire, and my own familiarity with Freire's work has not been surprising as a consequence of my exposure to his work. In fact, I also remember most vividly how I needed to conceal a copy of Freire's book out of fear of it being confiscated by the apartheid police as they roamed the streets in which my institution of study was located. What we as students feared most at the time, was being incarcerated for political reasons, and that our education would be untimely inhibited by a police force that had no credibility at the time. My personal encounter with Freire's *Pedagogy of the oppressed* (1970) was one of a deep attachment to his politically motivated transformative ideas. Of course, I would not consider myself a political activist during my high school years, but I was nevertheless politically aware to the extent that as a learner I led a protest march from my local high school in support of the 1976 Soweto revolts that witnessed black communities rise up against the compulsory introduction of the Afrikaans language in black schools. Afrikaans was considered by the majority of marginalised peoples at that time as a language of oppression, which advanced the political and educational interests of the then minority white ruling class. It was the same political awareness that would eventually make me connect with Freire's politico-educational ideas as a teacher in a local high school and, concurrently, as a post-graduate student at a local university. It was during these years that I read Freire's work in earnest. What made me connect with Freirean epistemology was both his call for education as liberation, and education as a pedagogy of caring.

Considered as his most important book, since *Pedagogy of the oppressed*, Freire's (2001) arguments for caring in *Pedagogy of freedom* accentuate three interrelated aspects that confirm his commitment to an openness to caring: firstly, Freire highlights the notion of caring towards students in relation to the practice of authentic teaching. In his words –

> This openness to caring for the well-being of the students does not mean of course that, I am obliged to care for all my students in the same way. What it does mean is that I am not afraid of my feelings and I know how to express myself effectively in an appropriate and affirming way. It also means I know how to fulfill authentically my commitment to my students in the context of a specifically human mode of action. (Freire, 2001: 125)

Such an authentic understanding of teaching enables teachers to awaken, stimulate and develop in students an attentiveness to learning that is critically reflective and theoretically rigorous (Freire, 2001: 128). When students become critically reflective, they are curious, bold and adventurous, willing 'to risk, to welcome the new' (Freire, 2001: 41). Students are no longer just prepared to accept things at face value; they give much thought to what they encounter. They are deeply cared for on the basis that their curiosity to find out things for themselves has been enhanced. Put differently, their potentialities have been evoked and they have become more open-minded because they do not fear what is new (Freire, 2001: 71).

Secondly, caring for students implies that teachers do not merely become methodologically rigorous in their questioning, but also more joyful and hopeful. By the latter, Freire (2001: 128) invokes the practice of acting in a therapeutic manner towards students when they happen to experience suffering or disquiet. Such a form of therapeutic caring is tantamount to acting with humanity towards students – that is, teachers' 'capacity for empathy and solidarity' with students who encounter vulnerable situations. When pedagogical encounters are constituted by caring, 'the exercise of productive thought and the development of the autonomy of both teachers and students [can be considered] ... a strictly human experience' (Freire, 2001: 129). Put differently, when teachers respect the autonomy of their students, they affirm respect for themselves. A teacher who cares for students respects their curiosity, questioning and freedom as fundamental to the human condition (Freire, 2001: 59). In Freire's words:

> Respect for the autonomy and dignity of every person is an ethical imperative and not a favour that we may or may not concede to each other. It is precisely because we are ethical beings that we can commit what can only be called a transgression by denying our essentially ethical condition. (Freire, 2001: 59)

Thus, following Freire, when students are provoked to act autonomously, they are cared for. A teacher who stimulates students' curiosity, questioning and freedom is a caring teacher – that is, an ethical teacher. Such a teacher is also aware that students are unfinished, curious and intelligent beings capable of struggling against the prejudices that prevent them from being human (Freire, 2001: 128). By implication, teachers who provoke students' capacities to think for themselves, act freely and combat human prejudices, can be said to care for students on the grounds that such students are stimulated to act autonomously. It is such an understanding of autonomy that evoked attitudes to undermine prejudice that characterised student activity at the university I attended. I remember several moments of conflict between students and lecturers whom the former perceived from their lectures as being too prejudicial. These lecturers were challenged and in some instances, such student–lecturer conflict erupted into mass marches on campus in the 1970s and 1980s.

Thirdly, caring is also related to the enactment of one's ethical responsibility (Freire, 2001: 127). For Freire (2001: 23), ethical responsibility involves the capacity developed in teachers and students to stand up for justice. When teachers and students act responsibly, they speak out against human misery, suffering, exploitation and manipulation of labour as well as racial, sexual and class discrimination (Freire, 2001: 23–24). According to Freire (2001: 24),

> The best way to struggle for this ethic [of caring] is to live it in our educative practice, in our relations with our students, in the way we deal with the contents of what we teach, and in this way we quote from authors – both those we agree with and those we do not.

It is the afore-mentioned idea of ethical caring that provoked me to support a teachers' march to the local police station in my early years as a teacher at a local high school. When the police arrested the entire learner population of the high school where I taught in the 1980s, on the grounds that our school was considered a volatile breeding ground for student political activists, some teachers and I did not hesitate to demonstrate our dissatisfaction in the face of apartheid police. Although, I would not say that our march eventually resulted in the police releasing the learners, I would assert that teachers' political awareness, including my own, had been enhanced by our politically troubled times instigated by police irrationality and at times, brutality. In a Freirean way, my own critically reflective capacity gained momentum as a consequence of my role as a teacher during the apartheid years. One could not have been a teacher from a historically disadvantaged community without having been conscientised with a profound political awareness during the apartheid years. In sum, following Freire, authentic caring involves the cultivation of our (teachers and students) critically reflective capacities; curiosity, freedom and sense of humanity; and our ethical responsibility within and beyond our pedagogical encounters, in much the same way as my early teaching experience brought on me. I now turn to a Freirean understanding of caring in relation to the seminal thoughts of Antonia Darder, Henry Giroux and Peter McLaren – three scholars who can be referred to as authentically Freirean in their thinking and practices.

Towards Enhancing Authentic Caring

The question this section addresses is how a Freirean notion of authentic caring could be commensurate with the seminal thoughts of neo-Freirean scholars such as Antonia Darder, Henry Giroux, and Peter McLaren. Firstly, Antonia Darder (2002: 179) makes a cogent case for integrating critical pedagogy in one's teaching. She has found that students she encountered often neglect to find a place for discussion, questioning and analysis within their interactions with both fellow students and teachers. She draws on Freire's idea of critical consciousness to nurture the cognitive and linguistic capacities of students in order that their critical voices be enhanced. In her words, 'conscientization, the development of critical consciousness, requires the ability to reflect and critique one's thoughts, actions, and motivations ... [in an] ongoing dialogue with peers and mentors' (Darder, 2002: 179). Through the cultivation of a Freirean critical consciousness, she hopes that some aspect of the lives of students and of teachers will be transformed to one that is more just (Darder, 2002: 180). In addition, Darder (2002: 181) posits that students in her classes learn that they have the potential to tell their stories and change their lives. In her words:

> My students were able to push each other through their supposed limitations and, through sustained effort, build and environment where it was safe to practice autonomy and self-regulation, critique each other's work and ideas, and propose changes to the teacher's plans. (Darder, 2002: 181)

Like Freire, Darder advocates an intent to develop the humility and patience to honour the capacity of our students – a matter of authentically caring for students (Darder, 2002: 89). She accentuates the Freirean notion to affirm our humanity in solidarity with students, and to transform the practices and structures within our educational institutions and society that produce human suffering (Darder, 2002: 87) – a clear indication of enhancing our ethical responsibility as humans. I, too, am attracted to Darder's Freirean approach to teaching. It is always important that students be conscientised into understandings of human suffering and exclusion so that they begin their intellectual projects with some sense of humanitarian awareness in mind. I cannot imagine students would engage in learning and be remiss of the inhumane situations that characterise societal living on the African continent without at least engaging with the conceptual underpinnings of such dilemmas and how to remedy it. Here, I specifically refer to initiating my students into thesis writing with the intent to ascertain how defensible understandings of democratic citizenship education potentially affect teaching and learning in higher education. Unless the intellectual programmes within which students are engaged are both conceptually and pragmatically linked to their own undesirable situations, say on the African continent, I cannot see how their learning would be of any humane and authentic concern. It consequently happens that my students ought to identify a pedagogical dilemma in their country of origin, and then set out to address such a predicament in their theses. As Darder intimates, students need to engage with their pedagogical narratives and then find ways to insert humanity into their critical intellectual work. The majority of my students at doctoral level who pursue a thesis in democratic citizenship education are required to show why and how such a form of education is relevant and transformative to education in their country of origin. Thereafter, they are also encouraged to examine, at least analytically, what the implications of such reconsidered notion of democratic citizenship education are for teaching and learning in their own contexts. At the time of writing this section, Mathalu Herbert Chikumbutso, a Malawian doctoral student, has just submitted his thesis on a reconsidered view of democratic citizenship education in Malawi and the implications of such an understanding for HE policy in Africa. The latter is an example of how students engage with an important concept and what the philosophical and educational implications of their studies offer education in Africa.

Secondly, Henry Giroux (2015: 116) offers an account of critical pedagogy that resonates with a Freirean notion of caring. For Giroux (2015: 116), critical pedagogy and by implication an education of care, aims 'to help students develop a consciousness of freedom, recognize authoritarian tendencies, empower the imagination, connect knowledge and truth to power, and learn how to read both the word and the world as part of a broader struggle of agency, justice, and democracy'. When teachers care for students, following Giroux (2015: 117), they make students aware that higher education has 'a deeply civic and political project that provides conditions for individual autonomy and takes liberation and practice of freedom as a collective goal'. In other words, to care for students in a Freirean way, implies that the individual autonomy of students is enhanced in relation to the passion for freedom and liberation on account that such a practice of caring 'offer[s] students the conditions for self-reflection, a self-managed life, and critical agency', (Giroux, 2015: 118). In other words, when teachers care, they contribute towards enhancing students' individual autonomy, which in turn, connects learning to social and political change (Giroux, 2015: 118). Moreover, like Freire and Darder, Giroux (2015: 118) accentuates the importance of engaging students in critical dialogue, criticism, and the cultivation of their ethical (social) responsibility towards others vis-à-vis self-reflection and 'a culture of questioning that demands far more than competency in rote learning and the application of acquired skills' (Giroux, 2015: 119). Put differently, caring through pedagogical encounters –

> [I]nsists that one of the fundamental tasks of educators is to make sure that the future points the way to a more socially just world, a world in which critique and possibility – in conjunction with the values of reason, freedom and equality – function to alter the grounds upon which life is lived. (Giroux, 2015: 119)

Thus, when teachers care for students, they are educated towards a future that is more hopeful and one that leads to freedom and social justice (Giroux, 2015: 120). Such an education becomes a responsibility also of students and teachers to make democratisation a possibility (Giroux, 2015: 121). By implication, Giroux equates such a Freirean pedagogy of caring with a pedagogy of bearing witness in the sense that students –

> [Become vigilant in] 'bearing witness to the individual and collective suffering of others … [and hence, caring teachers are urged to] the call for making the pedagogical more political with a continuing effort to build those coalitions, affiliations, and social movements capable of mobilizing real power and promoting substantive social change … to become critical agents alive to the responsibilities of democratic public life'. (Giroux, 2015: 122–123)

The post-apartheid university curriculum presented a challenge to many teachers and students. As a university teacher in the late 1990s, I was confronted with an intellectual challenge to move pedagogy away from its dominant apartheid legacy. I remember quite vividly how a democratic education project was taught through the agency of my departmental colleagues. Mostly, the idea of collective participation was accentuated as if participation alone would guarantee democratic engagement among teachers and students. My own involvement in curricular activities commenced in our department with an initiation into a different strand of democratic education. Whereas my department espoused a view of social democratic education in relation to people doing things together for the purpose of human development, my own pedagogical action was informed somewhat differently. I initiated students in an idea of democratic education that had an internal connection to freedom and emancipation – an idea of democratic education inclined towards the cultivation of human empowerment rather than just human development. It was during my early years of teaching that deliberative engagement gained much currency in the scholarly work I enacted in my department. Therefore, the inclusion of works of deliberative democratic theorists such as Amy Gutmann (1987), Seyla Benhabib (1992) and Eamonn Callan (1997) into our curriculum gained considerable momentum. At that stage, the democratic education curriculum was no longer just biased towards democratic participation, but rather moved keenly in the direction of deliberative engagement. At this juncture, it might be relevant to mention that, although my colleagues were not averse to deliberative democratic engagement, as university teachers initiated into conservative discourses of un-criticality and the lack of freedom to speak one's mind, they seemed hesitant to be drawn to deliberative inquiry that focused critical questioning and undermining of one another's perspectives. The point about adapting the democratic education curriculum in our department to some of the touchstones of deliberative engagement was that teachers and students in the then nascent post-apartheid era had the ethical responsibility to initiate one another into discourses of articulation, listening and talking back. Collective democratic participation alone cannot ensure enlarged moments of criticism and controversy. I sensed that democratic education during the nascent years of post-apartheid university education was merely an attempt at democratic positioning rather than an earnest pedagogical initiative to evoke more fractured and ruptured pedagogical encounters among students and teachers. Small wonder, deliberative democratic education theorists such as Gert Biesta, Penny Enslin, Nic Burbules, Tina Besley and Michael A. Peters were invited guests to our department in the early 2000s to teach on our democratic education curricular programme for mostly master's and doctoral students. In this way, deliberative democratic education seemed to have gained much currency in our departmental pedagogical initiatives. Of course, I would not say that the support in our department for deliberative democratic education was overwhelming; however, at least a different from of democratic education emerged, mostly associated with Anglo-Saxon philosophy of education at the time.

Thirdly, Peter McLaren (with Jenifer Crawford & Nana Gyamfi, 2009: 241) makes a case for an ethic of communal justice and care in the quest to advance equity within a community through education. Their argument is that prejudice such as racism, sexism and social injustice can most appropriately be undermined through a type of critical, liberatory education that is both relational and contextual (Crawford, Gyamfi, & McLaren, 2009: 249). As aptly stated by them:

Education has a duty to liberate where ... [learning] is neither fair nor just and the society does not present youth with equal opportunities to learn and to form positive relationships with self, community and society as a whole ... The simultaneous consideration of the needs of the individual and the community in the same ethical space defines the communal justice and care model of achieving the good.

Pursuant to the above, education for liberation requires care for those engaged in the encounter, which might result in students' individual as well as communal advancement. Moreover, coupled to an ethic of care and communal justice, teachers must actively identify and confront societal obstacles, such as racism, sexism, gender inequality and exclusion. And, most importantly, Crawford et al. (2009: 252) posit that an ethic of care is geared towards the cultivation of humanity in the sense that 'love, solidarity, respect, and willingness to address and redress the wrongs of society' should be cultivated. Put differently, an ethic of care – in the Freirean tradition – ought to guide educational encounters through which 'the struggle to end discrimination on the basis of race and gender and, sexual orientation' (Crawford et al., 2009: 252) will be enhanced. Of course, in relation to the democratic education curricular project I mentioned earlier, our department extended an invitation to African scholars in the diaspora with the intent to enhance deliberative politics through our intellectual work. Although only Kwase Wiredu (2005), the African philosopher from Atlanta in the United States came, his work nevertheless gave our pedagogical initiative a curricular impetus that later saw the introduction of African philosophy of education with a deliberative democratic education focus into our pedagogical initiatives. Wiredu (2005) brought to our department not just his leniency to African philosophy but most poignantly an understanding of integration that witnessed the fusion between an African philosophy of education reconsidered, and deliberative democratic education with an overwhelming concern towards redressing social injustices on the African continent in much the same way Crawford and his colleagues (2009) accentuated. This curricular change in our department signified an important academic initiative, namely that African philosophy of education could co-exist with an understanding of deliberative democratic education. Simply put, if African philosophy of education was identified as recognising major problems on the African continent followed by examining the implications of such analyses for education, then it would not be inappropriate to inquire what the implications are for deliberative democratic education. I concur that this is also a critical claim as many Anglo-Saxon philosophers of education opine that African philosophy of education cannot be reconciled with democratic education. If not, why is the view espoused that African philosophy of education is commensurable with social democracy? Nevertheless, Wiredu (2005) made me aware that African thought and practice do not have to be out of alignment with deliberative democratic education. In recognising the possibility of the latter view, it might just be possible to cultivate the notion of ethical care, which, in turn, links strongly with doing things in deliberation with others.

Summary

In this chapter, I offered an account of Freire's notion of authentic caring, which is inextricably linked to practices such as authentic learning, authoritative teaching, and the cultivation of ethical responsibility within pedagogical encounters. In addition, I have extended an explication of such an ethic of care that relates to Freire's critical pedagogy, which seems to be an entirely critically reflective, communal or dialogical, and ethically responsible endeavour most specifically related to the liberation of humanity and the advancement of just and humane interests within communities. At the very core of authentic caring is, once again, the idea that communal action ought to prevail. Simply put, for authentic care to manifest, humans ought to engage in some sort of transactional or pragmatic experience. In the next chapter, I look at the notion of transaction or pragmatic caring as enunciated in the works of Maurice Hamington and Dorothy Miller.

References

Benhabib, S. (1992). *Situating the self: Gender, community and postmodernism in contemporary ethics*. London: Polity Press.
Callan, E. (1997). *Creating citizens: Political education and liberal democracy*. Oxford, UK: Oxford University Press.

Crawford, J., Gyamfi, N., & McLaren, P. (2009). Unplaguing the stomach: Curing the University of California admissions policy with an ethic of communal justice and care. In H. S. Shapiro (Ed.), *Education and hope in troubled times: Visions of change for our children's world* (pp. 241–258). New York: Routledge.

Darder, A. (2002). *Reinventing Paulo Freire: A pedagogy of love*. Boulder, CO: Westview Press.

Freire, P. (1970). *Pedagogy of the oppressed*. London: Continuum.

Freire, P. (2001). *Pedagogy of freedom: Ethics, democracy, and civic courage*. Lanham, MD: Rowman & Littlefield.

Giroux, H. (2015). *Education and the crisis of public values: Challenging the assault on teachers, students, and public education* (2nd ed.). New York: Peter Lang.

Greene, M. (1995). *Releasing the imagination: Essays on education, the arts, and social change*. San Francisco, CA: Jossey-Bass.

Gutmann, A. (1987). *Democratic education*. Princeton, NJ: Princeton University Press.

Wiredu, K. (2005). Philosophical considerations on the Africanisation of higher education in Africa. In Y. Waghid (Ed.), *African(a) philosophy of education: Reconstructions and deconstructions* (pp. 6–18). Stellenbosch, South Africa: Stellenbosch University Printers.

4

Transactional or Pragmatic Caring: Enacting Care-Giving and Care Receiving

Introduction

In the previous three chapters, I have argued for a notion of caring that is inclusive, practical and authentic. At the centre of such explications of caring is the idea that people are in relationality, and the care on offer has some practical, social and political purpose in mind. Therefore, pedagogical encounters underscored by such notions of caring can be highly engaging, relational and politically driven, in much the same way as Carol Gilligan (1982), Nel Noddings (1984), and Paulo Freire (2001), respectively, have envisaged. Anecdotally speaking, I view my appointment in my current department two decades ago as one in which I also expected to be treated authentically with care, and that my transactional experiences with colleagues would manifest in relationships of care. Perhaps, I was somewhat naïve at the time to think that care would naturally unfold when humans in our department encountered one another academically and professionally. Little did I know at the time, that higher education can be a highly exclusivist activity where colleagues would not hesitate to make you feel somewhat unwelcome. I do not mention my initial induction into the department to show that not all academics had an inclination to care. However, I mention an incident below to show that transactional caring is a human experience that requires mutuality and engagement. One of my colleagues deemed it necessary to consider my appointment contentious. Understandably at the time, with not many people of colour having been appointed in the faculty, someone considered my appointment as other on the grounds of not belonging to the dominant culture at the time. When such conditions prevail, it seems very unlikely for collegiality to unfold and the possibility of mutual, transactional care might be curtailed. However, the senior professors in my department showed care, and my appointment never really became a public spat. My initiation into the department was supported by the recognition on the part of my senior colleagues that I could bring something else to the department. In a different way, the majority of my colleagues cared enough to recognise that democratic education would take on an extended form with my presence in the department. It is a notion of transactional care that interests me in the light of my own exposure to what I think happened with my appointment in the department where I still work. But first, I need to focus my attention specifically on what has emerged thus far as a non-individualistic notion of caring, in reference to the seminal thoughts of care ethicist, Maurice Hamington (2006), who specifically expounds on the care work of Jane Addams, in particular her work for the Hull-House caring settlement in Chicago, which lasted roughly from the late 1800s to World War I. What interests me about Hamington's work is his distinct focus on transactional caring as an instance of an ethic of care in relation to his exposition of socialising care (Hamington, 2006: 107).

Hamington's Analysis of Jane Addams's Work at Hull-House

Hamington (2006: 106) narrates the story of Hull-House, which began in 1889 with a small group of women activists who 'faced bleak social circumstances marked by widespread uncaring … [in] Chicago'. Many parts of the city were ruined by uncollected garbage and squalor, violence and injustice. Against the background of escalating immigration into Chicago, mostly without health, safety and labour laws prevalent at the time, two women, namely Jane Addams and Ellen Gates Starr founded the Chicago social settlement community known as Hull-House (Hamington, 2006: 107). In quite adequate detail, Hamington (2006: 107–108) describes the situation at the social settlement as follows:

> At their height, more than four hundred social settlements existed across the country. Hull-House rapidly assumed a leadership position among them because of the level of activity, innovation, and dynamism of its residents, particularly that of Jane Addams. From the beginning, Hull-House residents maintained a commitment to reciprocal relations among people of different identities. Addams believed that *society was made stronger through better understanding among diverse people*: "Hull-House was soberly opened on the theory that the dependence of classes on each other is reciprocal." Better knowledge of the rapidly growing immigrant population *would infuse new vitality and possibilities into the established culture* while facilitating the prosperity of those new to this country. The projects that Hull-House residents engaged in emerged from the transactions between its residents and the community. Hull-House would sponsor a public bathhouse, a kindergarten, child care, sex education programs, parks and recreation programs, a labor museum, adult education courses, social clubs, public speakers, community theater, and whatever else the community needed. (italics added)

Hamington uses the afore-mentioned example of Hull-House and the leadership and educational philosophy of Jane Addams (1860–1935) in particular, to give an account of transactional or pragmatic caring, which according to him, stretches beyond the seminal work of Nel Noddings. For him, Addams was a philosopher and feminist care ethicist, who used moral agency as constitutive of human interrelationships, unlike traditional theories on morality that enlist humans as atomistic individuals into relationships where they exert their autonomous rights vis-à-vis sympathy shown to others (Hamington, 2006: 108). In his words, 'Addams's robust approach to morality did not preclude rights and duties but she found a social ethic marked by care to be the missing voice of morality in the late nineteenth and early twentieth century' (Hamington, 2006:

110). Unlike Noddings who argues that care should be given to those who come into our proximity of knowledge, Addams, according to Hamington (2006: 110), considered caring as bringing others into one's proximal relationships and to care for them. 'Hull-House provided a sanctuary for women's independence and social separatism without the fetters of religious affiliation' (Hamington, 2006: 112).

I always thought that I was brought into a proximal relationship with my grandfather and grandmother who reared me until she died when I was six years old, and then my grandfather until his death when I was fifteen years old. My socialisation into the Muslim faith was done by my grandfather, commonly known as *'abu'* (that is, father). It was *abu* who later assumed a shortened version of *'bu'* who taught me to read the Quran – the primary source of Islam. For *bu*, as for the majority of Cape Muslims – who arrived from the Indonesian Archipelago in the late seventeenth century – the recitation of the Quran would not only protect me against any form of danger, but most of all, to become a committed Muslim, one has had to be knowledgeable of both Quranic reading and understanding. Small wonder, I already received a translation of the Quran as a gift in my teens. When I still browse through the same translated text, I can still identify the pencil marks underlying verses which *bu* wanted me to think about. It is quite interesting that at a very young age, my socialisation entailed both eloquence in Quranic recitation and occasional understanding of verses of relevance to my character development in my teens. Such an initiation into Muslim learning could only have happened on account of *bu's* eagerness and care to bring me into a transactional relationship with the Islamic faith. Before I share another aspect of my early learning, I offer my understanding of Hamington's account of transactional learning or pragmatic caring.

According to Hamington, 'at least six characteristics made up the socialized care that Hull-House employed to achieve so much success in local and later national reform'. These characteristics include proximity, listening, respect for others, willingness to act, fallibility, and flexibility (Hamington, 2006: 113). Thus, an ethic of care is inclusive, practical, authentic and, most importantly, it recognises the presence of human fallibilism. As aptly stated by Hamington (2006: 116):

> The goal of socializing care [transactional caring] is not perfection or some unrealistic moral world. The aim of socializing care is to create policies and institutions that value care through their attentiveness and responsiveness in a fundamentally human manner – which will entail mistakes.

The understanding of care Hamington espouses seems to extend the notions of caring developed in the first three chapters of this book, namely inclusive, practical and authentic caring. Pragmatic or transactional caring seems to be 'a communal culture of care that sought to employ sympathetic understanding to local issues … [such as] fighting for garbage collection, establishing juvenile courts, creating playgrounds for children, and dispensing birth control information' (Hamington, 2006: 117). If one contextualises such a notion of caring within pedagogical encounters, then it does not seem adequate enough that teachers listen respectfully to the views of students and then relate their caring in a Freirean way to the liberation of some political activity beyond the university class. Rather, pragmatic caring also recognises the fallibility of both students and teachers as they endeavour to transform undesirable practices in their social world. It is the recognition that those engaged in the pedagogical encounter might err and should be recognised for their fallibility and not prematurely be excluded on the grounds that they (for instance, students) should always get things right. Pragmatic caring is a recognition that students should be cared for in the sense that the mistakes they make should not be used to emasculate them. An ethic of care that is inclusive, practical, authentic and transactional could go some way in 'creating the opportunity for understanding, trust, and responsiveness' (Hamington, 2006: 114) to the marginalised students within pedagogical encounters. Inasmuch as my grandfather, *bu* continued to socialise me into the Muslim faith, his teaching approach was somewhat different from a recognition of human fallibility. He clearly did not tolerate that I made mistakes during my Quranic recitation and would, at times, harshly dismiss my recitation. Perhaps, in the community I was reared, errors in recitation were always used to ridicule people. And, for the latter reason, *bu's* belligerence is quite understandable. However, inasmuch as he cared, his caring seemed to have been restricted to an accentuation of proximity at the expense of recognising fallibilism. I am by no means implying that his caring was deficient. Only that, his caring for me was incommensurable with any notion of recognising humans as fallible. Yet, I witnessed fallibility in his home. But, when it came to me, I dare not to have erred otherwise his attitude towards me would have changed instantly. No wonder, he decided that I should attend a local *madrassa* (Muslim school) because he could no longer deal with my fallibility in relation to my Muslim learning.

In relation to the idea of recognising fallibilism as constitutive of transactional caring, I am reminded of the discipline of Philosophy of Education that I teach to post-graduate students. Often it appeared as if some students did not respond too well to an initiation into concepts such as 'dissonance' and 'cosmopolitanism'. In such cases, I would listen to what students had to say about their understandings of such concepts. Yet, I would not prematurely judge their understandings considering that they might be affronted and, by implication, possibly withdraw from the encounter. This is what I have learned when I attended the local *madrassah*. My teacher would listen attentively to my recitation without abruptly correcting my mistakes. After he had listened to my recitation, he would advise me to repeat the verses that were identified as having been pronounced incorrectly and requested that I repeat those verses. And when he heard the mistakes again, he would then point out to me where and why I had erred. This kind of supportive learning formed the thrust of my approach to teaching as a pragmatic carer. At times, I would listen to Philosophy of Education students' unjustifiable views, without pointing out their mistakes. I would allow them to make those mistakes only with the possibility that they might recognise their own mistakes in the light of ongoing conversations about concepts in class. In support of such a view, Alasdair MacIntyre (1999: 144, emphasis added) aptly reminds us:

> [When teachers and students engage in] the exercise of shared deliberative rationality [it] is always imperfect and what should impress us is not so much the *mistakes* made and the limitations upon its exercise at any particular stage as the ability through time and conflict to correct those mistakes and to move beyond those limitations [by ourselves].

The point MacIntyre (1999: 136) makes is that caring for students cannot just be about the prevalence of theoretical reflection and to stand hastily in judgement of others (students). What is central to pedagogical encounters is the recognition that teachers and students are dependent on one another, and the exercise of critical judgement cannot be free from error otherwise participants in such encounters will not have the courage to take risks (MacIntyre, 1999: 92). In other words, through transactional caring, teachers and students, in MacIntyre's (1999: 92, italics added) words:

> [Know] when to take risks and when to be cautious, when to delegate a task to others and when to take it one oneself, when to be generous with deserved praise and *sparing of deserved blame,* when to be exacting whether with oneself or with others and when to be more relaxed, when a joke is needed and when anger is appropriate.

To come back to Hamington's (2006) idea of pragmatic care, it is also worthwhile to point out two aspects: first, that a community will turn out to be 'stronger through better understanding of diverse people'. In much the same way, our department became academically stronger with more diverse appointments, so understanding of democratic education was also expanded. Second, diversity infuses 'new vitality and possibilities into the established culture' (Hamington, 2006: 117). A culture of exclusion and marginalisation in our department evolved into multiple possibilities that considered alternative understandings of democratic education. As mentioned earlier in this chapter, the notion of an African philosophy of education that gained prominence in our department is an expansion of our deliberative engagement with new thoughts and ideas. Colleagues and I were prepared to take more risks as we endeavoured to construct and reconstruct defensible understandings of a reconsidered view of democratic education. We became engaged in a practice of pragmatic caring.

The aforementioned discussion on transactional or pragmatic caring brought to the fore that caring itself manifests in multiple ways. Cheryl Brandsen (2006) identifies at least four approaches to caring: firstly, when people care about others they do so on the basis of being in attendance to others, such as when others are in need of care (Brandsen, 2006: 206). Caring about others is therefore both an individual and a collective ethical activity in the sense that '[t]he ethical aspect that attaches to the phase of "caring about" is attentiveness. Attentiveness is required to recognize that there is a need about which to be concerned' (Brandsen, 2006: 206). Secondly, Brandsen posits, 'taking care of' implies that one or a group take the responsibility to act in the interest of the needs of others, such as taking care of other through investing one's time, money and skills to respond to a need (Brandsen, 2006: 206). Thus whereas 'caring about' others is a practice which involves actually being in attendance of others, one does not have the responsibility to do so. Assuming the responsibility of caring for others, obliges one to 'taking care of them'. In other words, 'caring about' seems to be associated with the exercise of voluntary acts, whereas 'taking responsibility for' obliges one to act for others. Thirdly, 'care-giving' is linked to the moral competence one exercises in giving care to others in need. According to Brandsen (2006: 207), '[t]ypically this is the physical, "hands-on" work of care, and usually involves direct contact with care receivers … To demonstrate that one cares, caring work needs to be performed competently.' Fourthly, 'care receiving' is mostly associated with the responsiveness of the care receivers to the care-givers' concern to care. For Brandsen (2006: 207),

> The moral aspect of caring that attaches to the phase of "care receiving" is responsiveness. Because care is concerned with experiences of vulnerability and inequality, responsiveness requires that caregivers remain alert to the possibilities for abuse that arise with vulnerability.

Now, it is my understanding that pedagogical encounters among teachers and students mostly involve pragmatic 'care-giving' and 'care receiving'. Teachers as care-givers use their pedagogical authority to address students' learning deficiencies in a competent manner. Likewise, students as care receivers become responsive to the care given by teachers on account of their (the students') vulnerabilities perhaps not to grasp elucidations of teachers adequately. The notions of 'care-giving' and 'care receiving' enacted on the part of teachers and students respectively enhance the pedagogical encounters as activities that can be intellectually rigorous. When pedagogical encounters are sufficiently well informed on account of 'care-giving' and 'care receiving', teachers and students can enhance 'their capacity to imagine alternative futures, and their disposition to recognize and to make true practical judgements concerning a variety of goods' (MacIntyre, 1999: 96). And, what makes pragmatic or transactional caring fallible is that at any point we might go astray 'in our practical reasoning because of intellectual error' on account that we (teachers and students) might perhaps remain 'insufficiently well informed about the particulars of our situation ... or we have relied too heavily on some unsubstantiated generalization' (MacIntyre, 1999: 96). Perhaps, my personal encounters at a *madrassah* might have stimulated in me a desire to care when teachers recognise the fallibility of learners and, unlike my grandfather, would not always choose to reprimand us (learners). Of course, I am not intimating that all learning at *madrassah* was as caring as the way I described thus far. What should also be emphasised is that rote learning practices seemed to have dominated *madrassah* learning. However, even when rote learning was the dominant way of learning there was always the possibility of transactional care to manifest in *madrassah* practices.

Summary

In this chapter, I have given some account of transactional or pragmatic caring by drawing on Maurice Hamington's analysis of the Hill-House community settlement. For Hamilton (2006), as for Jane Addams, pragmatic caring involves listening to and respecting others in an atmosphere of willing action whereby fallibility on the part of students is clearly taken into account as teachers endeavour to exercise their care. When university teachers exercise their care towards students, they listen attentively to what students have to say, they respect the judgements of their students, and they recognise holding back on their judgements of students' work so that students can come to their autonomous understandings without always being corrected or told by teachers what to do. That is, teachers recognise the fallibility of students to make mistakes and do not prematurely and/or hastily judge their articulations. Teachers create a pedagogical atmosphere of inclusion where students can, first of all, rectify their own faults without having to be reprimanded by teachers for their errors. In this way, caring would be highly transactional or pragmatic. That is, teachers and students as care-givers and care receivers engage competently in pedagogical encounters and urge one another to speak with clarity and intellectual rigour to the extent that they become immersed in their speech acts without prematurely judging one another's perspectives. It is through pragmatic or transactional caring that the potentiality for alternative views is always possible because of the recognition that human intellectual fallibility is never dismissed as not being part of pedagogical encounters.

References

Brandsen, C. (2006). A public ethic of care: Implications for long-term care. In M. Hamington & D. C. Miller (Eds.), *Socializing care: Feminist ethics and public issues* (pp. 205–226). Lanham, MD: Rowan & Littlefield.
Freire, P. (2001). *Pedagogy of freedom: Ethics, democracy, and civic courage.* Lanham, MD: Rowman & Littlefield.
Gilligan, C. (1982). *In a different voice: Psychological theory and women's development.* Cambridge, MA: Harvard University Press.
Hamington, M. (2006). An inverted home: Socializing care at Hull-House. In M. Hamington & D. C. Miller (Eds.), *Socializing care: Feminist ethics and public issues* (pp. 105–120). Lanham, MD/Boulder, CO/New York/Toronto, ON/Oxford, UK: Rowman & Littlefield Publishers.
MacIntyre, A. (1999). *Dependent rational animals: Why human beings need the virtues.* London: Duckworth.
Noddings, N. (1984). *Caring: A feminine approach to ethics and moral education.* Berkeley, CA: University of California Press.

5

Attentive Caring: On Coming into Presence Within Pedagogical Encounters

Introduction

In this chapter, I focus my attention on Selma Sevenhuijsen's (2018) explication of attention vis-à-vis an ethic of care. Following Sevenhuijsen, a care ethicist, pedagogical encounters would be unthinkable without attention. In all four notions of caring discussed in the previous chapter (i.e. caring about, taking care of, care-giving and care receiving), the idea of attention was prominent, in the sense that caring cannot exist without the practice of attending to oneself and others. Sevenhuijsen's claim is that 'practising active attention starts with our self, with a willingness to reflect on our own actions and reactions, with the intention to improve the quality of our caring interactions with others' (Sevenhuijsen, 2018: 3). It is such a self-activity of attentive caring that I shall discuss in relation to pedagogical encounters.

On Being Attentive

In the previous chapter, I have shown in relation to Maurice Hamington's idea of caring that human fallibilism ought to be recognised on the part of care-givers and care receivers. And, considering that care receivers who are cared for would not be prematurely and harshly judged for their mistakes, it makes sense to speak about caring constitutive of transactional relationships. In other words, care receivers would be cared for when care-givers recognise the capacity of the former to err and by implication would not be callously judged for the mistakes they have made. Although Selma Sevenhuijsen (2018: 3) would not be averse to such an idea of transactional caring, she avers that caring has both a purpose and intention with which it is provided – that is, caring is an act of attention. For Sevenhuijsen (2018: 3) –

> [A]ttention is an activity that is aimed at human flourishing … [and] practicing active attention starts with our self, with a willingness to reflect on our own actions and reactions, with the intention to improve the quality of our caring interactions with others.

According to Sevenhuijsen (2018: 3), caring as attention or attentive caring comprises a 'waiting' and 'holding' dimension. Firstly, the 'waiting' dimension of attention 'refers to the need to suspend one's own suppositions, images and preoccupations when engaging in a caring interaction' (Sevenhuijsen, 2018: 3). In other words, when teachers attend to students, they engage in waiting where they see the students as they are and could be. That is, teachers should be able to see both the actuality and potential of their students who remain in becoming. Secondly, when teachers engage in the 'holding' dimension of attentive caring they attend well to students and suspend and hold back their own feelings, attachments and 'fixed ideas' to acknowledge the otherness within their students. Whereas the waiting aspect of attentive care involves 'taking time before engaging in over hastened or unreflected forms of need-interpretation … [holding makes us] able to reach out to others … and be attentive to what is happening inside us' (Sevenhuijsen, 2018: 5). Put differently, if teachers want to take care of students they have to develop 'an active will for inner growth … [such as] the overcoming of inner barriers for change and dealing with complex – often repressed – emotions like sorrow, anger, fear, aggression and despair' (Sevenhuijsen, 2018: 5).

I am specifically thinking of the Arabic dictum, *'man 'arafa nafsahu qadd 'arafa rabbahu'* – whoever knows himself or herself, knows his or her Lord (al-Attas, 1993b: 69). For many Arab and Muslim peoples all over the world, this Arabic expression is quite significant in the sense that learning starts with what Sevenhuijsen (2018: 5) refers to as caring for the soul. According to al-Attas (1993b: 18), knowing the self implies that meanings of things have arrived in the soul. In other words, a caring soul is one that is imbued with knowledge, which in turn is infused with wisdom (*hikmah*) and justice (*adl*) and, contribute towards goodness (*adab*) within the individual self (al-Attas, 1993b: 22–23). In this regard, al-Attas (1993a: 25) posits that disciplining the soul – what I would interpret as caring for the soul – potentially produces a good person who in turn contributes to the goodness (justice) of society. Consequently, al-Attas (1993b: 34) avers that a loss of soul is tantamount to the loss of the capacity for discernment and to see things in their appropriate places. This makes sense on the basis that not caring for the soul could lead to injustices within the HE system (al-Attas, 1993a: 38). Thus, when pedagogical encounters do not recognise the importance of caring for the soul of teachers and students, such encounters would remain inattentive and unengaging for that matter. When I visited the International Institute of Islamic Thought and Civilisation (ISTAC) in Kuala Lumpur in the 1990s as a post-doctoral fellow, on invitation from its director, Prof. Wan Muhammad Nor Wan Daud, I was exposed to learning from an Islamic perspective. What I constantly encountered through the lectures of its founder, Prof. Syed Muhhamad Naquib al-Attas, was that learning ought to be induced through *adab* – goodness – which students have to internalise in order for them to acquire wisdom and knowledge. In other words, during my time at ISTAC, I experienced a profound accentuation of caring for the soul before knowledge, as it was taught, could be made sense of. The point is that, for Muslim scholars, the acquisition of knowledge is conditional upon an attentiveness to the soul. That makes sense, because caring for the soul invokes in one an earnestness to pursue higher education. Consequently, one finds that when post-graduate students are initiated into an understanding of knowledge, they are reminded – during their introduction to learning – to be attentive to their souls – a matter of becoming persons of *adab*. Therefore, it is not surprising that al-Attas (1993a) blames the decline of higher education in the Arab and Muslim world, as a result of a lack of *adab*, or an inattentiveness to the soul. Next, I address the question how pedagogical encounters would unfold if they were to function on the basis of attentive caring.

Attentive Pedagogical Encounters

Based on the afore-mentioned notion of attentive caring, I now offer an account of three democratic moments that could be opened up within university pedagogical encounters. Firstly, when teachers and students engage in attentive pedagogical encounters, they recognise one another as being in the present – that is, they are 'there' and not absent from the encounter. When both teachers and students are present, they care about the matters under consideration – that is, they are both inspired by the lesson and want to learn from one another's understandings of the lesson. If teachers and students are not present, teaching and learning would not materialise. The actuality that teachers teach means that they are in the presence of students who are expected to learn. In other words, bringing teachers and students into the presence of teaching and learning respectively, is a condition of democratic education. In this way, caring would hopefully be in attention. The point about teachers bringing students into the present has to do with bringing the curricular matter into 'contact' with students who are expected to be 'touched' by it – in other words, teachers bring curricula matters 'near' to students (Masschelein & Simons, 2011: 162).

Secondly, when teachers are attentive in care to students, there is already an implicit assumption on the part of teachers that when they bring a curriculum matter to students, the students are able to make sense of what they are being taught. As aptly put by Masschelein and Simons (2011: 162), when teachers bring students into presence, 'they [students] come to their senses … [a]nd the lesson can only start at the moment that the burden of inability falls away'. Following this line of thought, the university is the place where our knowledge and capabilities are enacted unconstrainedly within pedagogical encounters.

Thirdly, when teachers attentively care for students, they actually 'give all students new chances over and over again' (Masschelein & Simons, 2011: 163). This means that students are not left to their own devices but rather, caring teachers ask 'for attention from students' (Masschelein & Simons, 2011: 163). In this way, teachers 'make the experience of a new use [of curricular knowledge] possible at all [as a consequence of] love for the world and the new generation' (Masschelein & Simons, 2011: 163). As a consequence of such an understanding of pedagogical encounters, Sevenhuijsen (2018: 7–8) is right when she associates attentive caring with the cultivation of presence, discernment and having trust and honour in our students.

Considering such an explication of attentive caring, I am still baffled by the then Malaysian government's decision to curb the intellectualism of ISTAC and its founder-director, Professor al-Attas. ISTAC was incorporated into the Faculty of Education at the International Islamic University of Malaysia and its founder-director was put on premature retirement. Ever since, ISTAC, considered by its proponents as a 'beacon on the crest of a hill' never lived up to its status of an attentively caring HEI, primarily because an advancement of presence, knowledge and discernment never really remained associated with the institute. The point is, political intervention seemed to have derailed the scholarly intensions of an illustrious institute of learning. It is not so much the curtailment of knowledge but more importantly, the opportunity for scholars to have acquired the appropriate care to pursue their intellectual advances that was dealt a heavy blow.

Summary

In sum, attentive caring offers opportunities for both teachers and students to be in one another's presence through which they can exercise the capacities to make sense of what is being presented to them. In addition, being attentive through caring also affords participants to use their chances to come to understanding about what is known and what is still to come. In a different way, attentive caring within pedagogical encounters creates opportunities for students to engage in what Gert Biesta (2011: 34) refers to as a pedagogy without explanation. Such a pedagogy allows students to learn for themselves because they have been brought into attention by teachers. According to Biesta (2011: 35), through a pedagogy without explanation, students 'can see and think for themselves and are not dependent upon others [teachers] who claim that they can see and think for them [students]'. In other words, through a pedagogy without explanation, teachers are answerable and attentive to students without always instructing them (the students) what to think and do.

References

Al-Attas, S. M. N. (1993a). *Islam and secularism*. Kuala Lumpur, Malaysia: International Institute of Islamic Thought and Civilisation.

Al-Attas, S. M. N. (1993b). *The concept of education in Islam: A framework for an Islamic philosophy of education*. Kuala Lumpur, Malaysia: International Institute of Islamic Thought and Civilisation.

Biesta, G. (2011). Learner, student, speaker: Why it matters how we call those we teach. In J. Masschelein & M. Simons (Eds.), *Rancière, public education and the taming of democracy* (pp. 31–42). Oxford, UK: Wiley-Blackwell.

Masschelein, J., & Simons, M. (2011). The hatred of public schooling: The school as the mark of democracy. In J. Masschelein & M. Simons (Eds.), *Rancière, public education and the taming of democracy* (pp. 150–165). Oxford, UK: Wiley-Blackwell.

Sevenhuijsen, S. (2018). Care and attention. *South African Journal of Higher Education, 32*(6), 1–14.

6

Democratic Caring: Building Relations of Freedom, Equality and Emancipation

Introduction

Considering that my own work has mostly involved the cultivation of democratic citizenship education in (South) Africa, any notion of care linked to the idea of democracy invariably gripped my attention. It is in this context, that I encountered Joan Tronto's work as relevant to my scholarship. Joan Tronto (2013: 140, 146), a political scientist and caring ethicist, endorses the views that care is relational, and 'to become more caring is to become more attentive and more capable of making judgements about responsibility'. At face value, her understanding of care does not seem different from those articulated by Gilligan, Noddings, Freire, Hamington and Sevenhuijsen, as articulated in the previous chapters. However, in her book, entitled, *Caring democracy*, Tronto (2013) makes three pertinent moves that suggest that caring involves more than just relationality, attentiveness and responsibility. In this chapter, I consider what she means by democratic caring, and I show how she is perhaps too presumptuous in dismissing dyadic care, particularly in relation to a teacher and student. In the main, for Tronto (2013), democratic caring ought to be seen as caring *with* others, which is different from caring *about* and caring *for* others – a view that, as I show, resonates with my own understanding of democratic pedagogical encounters.

Towards Democratic Caring

Tronto (2013: 140) avers that caring in a democratic society is highly participatory and, at the least, depends on the legitimate inclusion of all citizens. If caring is participatory, then it has to be inclusive in the first instance. And, if it involves 'everyone's perspectives' as Tronto (2013: 140) posits, then such a form of caring implies that all citizens' voices have to find some form of representation in such a society. In her words –

> [D]emocratic politics should center upon assigning responsibilities for care, and for ensuring that democratic citizens are as capable as possible of participating in this assignment of responsibilities for care ... Democratic citizens are all engaged in [relations] provided and need care together; this *caring with* is a political concern and one that needs to be resolved through politics. (Tronto, 2013: 140, original italics)

My interest is in Tronto's claim that democratic citizens 'are all engaged in ... care together' (2013: 153). She further substantiates being in 'care together' on the basis of democratic citizens exercising their capacities of freedom, equality and justice. Firstly, regarding pedagogical encounters, when teachers and students exercise their freedom, they are not inhibited by others to speak their minds. In other words, the pedagogical authority of a teacher is not sufficient justification to curtail students' free speech acts. As corroborated by Tronto (2013: 153), 'democratic caring concerns the breaking down of hierarchical relationships'. That is, both teachers and students have a pedagogical autonomy to say what comes to mind and thus open up their views firmly for critical scrutiny by one another. Learning cannot unfold if students are curtailed to articulate their rational judgements freely. Similarly, teaching would be constrained if teachers were to be inhibited to speak their minds. Thus, at the centre of democratic caring is the practice that both teachers and students are speaking beings. Gert Biesta (2011: 39) distinguishes learners from students. He posits when we refer to subjects in education as learners, we immediately put them in a position of dependence on teachers for their learning. But, when we refer to those who are the subject of education as students, we begin from the assumption that they can learn without teachers' explanations. That is, in a Rancièrean way, students are emancipated and free – a matter of students having the capacity to speak (Biesta, 2011: 39). In this regard, Biesta (2011: 39) posits the following:

> Emancipatory [free] education can therefore be characterized as education that starts from the assumption that all students can speak – or to be more precise: that all students can *already* speak. It starts from the assumption that students neither lack a capacity for speech, nor that they are producing noise. It starts from the assumption, in other words, that students are already *speakers*.

And, when students can already speak, they can also make sense of curriculum matters. That is, they do not need to be explained this or that matter. Rather they have the capacity to interpret, understand and articulate as speaking beings. As speaking beings, students can contribute towards the democratic conversation and, thus, can also care with teachers for both parties.

Secondly, democratic caring, following Tronto, is constituted by equality and this, she intimates, ought to be exercised in a manner that undermines hierarchical relationships. I agree with Tronto and want to extend this view of cultivating equal relationships among students and teachers in reference to the seminal thoughts of Jacques Rancière (2000). For Rancière (2000), equality refers to an assumption that teachers and students are all able to do this or that. Such an idea of equality does not refer to having equal opportunities or qualifications. Instead, for Rancière (2000), equality is always intellectual equality, namely an ability on the part of all students and teachers to speak and understand. Thus, equality refers to an assumption that teachers and students are all equal regardless of their qualifications and/or opportunities. For Rancière (2000: 3), equality is therefore not given to someone but rather, equality is assumed as a point of departure on the part of those who come to speech. Thus, when teachers engage with students they recognise the equal intelligence of students to come to speech – that is, of being able to intervene. As Biesta (2011: 35) avers, equality 'is to remind people that they can see and think for themselves and are not dependent upon others who claim that they can see and think for them'.

Thirdly, Tronto (2013) considers democratic justice as constitutive of caring. For Rancière (2007), democratic justice is enacted through an assumption of equality on the part of participants, say students within pedagogical encounters, whereby they ably disrupt or reconfigure such encounters. In other words, teachers and students are both capable of disrupting pedagogical encounters on account of their equal capacities to speak. For Rancière (2016), disruption refers to as the cultivation of dissensus among participants within encounters. And, the emergence of dissensus within encounters is a vindication that not everyone sees matters in exactly the same way. As aptly put by Rancière (2016: 146–147) –

> [Dissensus or disagreement] is the affirmation of their [students and teachers] capacity to reconstruct their world of experience, therefore to take their part in the global reconfiguration of the social world ... They work by disrupting the way in which bodies fit their functions and destinations ... they produce a multiplicity of folds and gaps in the fabric of common experience that change the cartography of the perceptible, the thinkable, and the feasible.

Put differently, a democratic justice underscored by care summons participants (students and teachers) to exercise their equality to produce dissensus that has the potential to disrupt the taken-for-granted and the established because 'there is a capacity for thinking that does not belong to any special group, a capacity that can be attributed to anybody' (Rancière, 2016: 150). This brings me to a discussion of why dyadic care, as Tronto suggests, should not be so easily dismissed. The afore-mentioned understanding of democratic caring reminds me of 'writing for publication' workshops I conducted at several historically disadvantaged universities in South Africa. In an attempt to show how democratic caring can work, I refer to a workshop of this kind I presented at the Limpopo University at the time of authoring this book (June 2018). As a corroboration of democratic caring, participants and I concurred that the rationale for our publication workshop ought to be 'decoloniality, love and care, and transformation'. Our reason for choosing decoloniality, related to moving beyond some of the firmly entrenched traditions of doing educational research at the institution's faculty of education, most notably, positivistic inquiry into pedagogical matters. Of course, it is quite challenging to instantly trump firmly entrenched traditions of educational inquiry if, for many years, such paradigms of research have been practiced in an unchallenged way. And, if educational research seemed to have been confined to providing 'solutions' to pedagogical concerns, through cause–effect strategies, academics would be reluctant initially to accept change. Hence, it was not surprising when I heard from many group members that they are attracted to positivistic inquiry. Of course, as I rightly pointed out to the group, positivistic inquiry might have its merits; however, when decoloniality is at play, educational researchers would hardly find comfort in the tenets of verification, objectivity, manipulation, standardisation, control and prediction. As a consequence, I found several members of the group's dogmatic allegiance to positivism quite alarming to say the least. Positivistic educational inquiry is not a plausible research paradigm that can deal adequately with the cultivation of notions, such as decoloniality, love and care, and transformation, primarily as a result of the apolitical, asocial and ahumanistic stances of positivistic inquiry. Despite our belligerent forms of engagement at times, our desire to express our equality was a vindication that participants in the workshop were not prepared to be silenced, and even some of their equal articulations in defence of positivistic inquiry, corroborated the justification that democratic caring was at play. However, what I found surprisingly absent from the deliberations among them was a tenable justification why educational research ought to be concerned with transformation. I am by no means intimating that participants saw no need to transform HE practices. Rather, their justification for educational transformation was somewhat inattentive. The point about educational transformation of the HE system in South Africa ought to be considered by academics as an ethical responsibility, if workshops such as 'writing for publication' were to be meaningful at all. And, for such educational development opportunities to manifest and remain credible, participants ought to couple their scholarly work with an enhancement of ethical responsibility. Only then can decoloniality, love and care, and transformation influence our scholarly work more intelligently. The point is that democratic caring has to manifest in every facet of our transformative work. This brings me to an important matter Tronto raises in her defence of democratic caring.

In Defence of Dyadic Care

Tronto (2013: 153) is adamant that the logic of dyadic care is not commensurate with democratic caring on the basis that the former involves a one-on-one relationship whereas the latter involves the participation of many. Following Tronto (1993: 156), the 'dyadic model of care is not only inaccurate, it is also normatively not a good model of care. Care, like other aspects of human life, benefits from being done by more people'. Supervision of post-graduate students is an example of dyadic care in the sense that such a pedagogical action involves a supervisor and a student. To assume that a supervisor cannot be as committed to a student as he or she should be and to assume that a supervisor also cannot be attuned to a student and by implication care for the student, is just an erroneous assumption. If a supervisor cannot be said to care for a student, then the possibility that the supervisor might not be responsive to a student is also possible.

However, as I have argued elsewhere, supervisors can be responsive to a student's work, and by implication also be in solidarity with such student — that is, it is quite possible to have a relationship of trust between a supervisor and a student (Waghid, 2015). In a previous work, *Dancing with doctoral encounters: Democratic education in motion* (Waghid, 2015), I narrate the stories of fifteen encounters I had with doctoral students. Although my caring can be said to have been dyadic, in no way were my encounters with the students inattentive and undemocratic. Instead, my doctoral encounters can be equated to a rhythmic dance, as I offered advice and also allowed students to articulate themselves as my own voice became less and less significant. The point is, a supervisor can respond to a student on account of engaging in a relationship of care with the student. In this way, dyadic caring might not be as inaccurate and untrustworthy as Tronto assumes. And, considering that a dyadic relationship can also be highly provocative and deliberative, there is always the possibility and pedagogical space for a student to talk back to a supervisor by articulating his or her points of view in a thesis which the supervisor invariably considers plausible or not. In this regard, even in a one-on-one relationship between a supervisor and a student, democratic politics can be at play. There is sufficient opportunity for the student and the supervisor to deliberate, thus allowing for articulation, listening and talking back to one another, comprising those touchstones of deliberative engagement that make democratic caring highly likely to occur in dyadic pedagogical relations between a student and a supervisor. Considering that a supervisor shares a common purpose with a student, it is very unlikely to assume that such a form of dyadic care would not be a form of authentic democratic caring. The point is that dyadic caring is still a matter of caring *with* others. Therefore, if I understand Tronto correctly, it is not plausible to undermine dyadic caring prematurely. Dyadic caring is constitutive of democratic caring. Without dyadic relationships, democratic engagement and, by implication, caring would be absent from pedagogical encounters. Yet, by far the most poignant reason why student–supervisor relationships ought to be constituted by democratic caring, is because such a notion of caring does not unfold without a political intent. Consequently, as I have alluded to earlier in my discussion of educational development vis-à-vis publication workshops, ethical and political responsibility ought to emanate from our experiences of democratic caring. Only then does higher education stand a chance of being transformed with care. The moment of care would have been ruptured on account of democratic caring.

Summary

Democratic caring involves participants – teachers and students – who act freely, equally and disruptively within pedagogical encounters. In this way, Tronto's (2013) notion of caring *within* offers more than just inclusive, practical, authentic, transactional and attentive caring. I have made a case for democratic caring as a politico-educational act of justice. Without it, higher education, certainly in developing countries like South Africa, would miss the chance to transform authentically and caringly.

References

Biesta, G. (2011). Learner, student, speaker: Why it matters how we call those we teach. In J. Masschelein & M. Simons (Eds.), *Rancière, public education and the taming of democracy* (pp. 31–42). Oxford, UK: Wiley-Blackwell.

Rancière, J. (2000). Literature, politics, aesthetics: Approaches to democratic disagreement. *SubStance, 29*(2), 3–24.

Rancière, J. (2007). *The politics of aesthetics: The distribution of the sensible* (G. Rockhill, Trans.). London, UK: Continuum.

Rancière, J. (2016). Critical questions on the theory of recognition. In K. Genel & J. P. Deranty (Eds.), *Recognition or disagreement: A critical encounter on the politics of freedom, equality, and identity* (pp. 83–95). New York: Columbia University Press.

Tronto, J. (1993). *Moral boundaries: A political argument for an ethic of care.* London, UK: Routledge.

Tronto, J. (2013). *Caring democracy: Markets, equality, and justice.* New York: New York University Press.

Waghid, Y. (2015). *Dancing with doctoral encounters: Democratic education in notion.* Stellenbosch, South Africa: Sun Press.

7

Empathic Caring

Introduction

When, I first planned this book, I thought that democratic caring would be the highlight of this book, considering that my intellectual work deals with democratic education. My concern is always what other forms caring could assume if democratic caring already integrates multiple notions of caring, as discussed throughout this book. Only when I read Michael Slote's work on caring did I realise that democratic caring might not be an overarching enough term for notions of care that deal with virtues of compassion, forgiveness and reconciliation – aspects of educational inquiry that feature prominently in my writings on educational justice. Thus, in this chapter, I draw on the seminal work of Michael Slote (2007) to elucidate a notion of empathic caring. I argue that such a notion of caring is commensurate with an enactment of respect and dignity towards others. Likewise, I show how respect and dignity as manifestations of empathic care could influence pedagogical encounters positively. Then, I look at the notion of justice and how empathic care could enhance just pedagogical relationships through an emphasis on constraining injurious speech.

First, however, I narrate an encounter with my daughter, Sihan, a medical doctor working as a registrar dermatologist at a local public hospital. When she heard that I am writing a book on caring in education, she was somewhat surprised because she thought that the medical profession is about the only authentic profession that deals justifiably with the notion of caring for patients. When I asked her about the care for medical practitioners, she was somewhat bemused again because as she asserted, her work involves providing care to those in need. Seemingly oblivious of the fact that care-givers can also be care recipients, and that care is not a practice strictly confined to the medical profession, she raised an important aspect of what seems to be wrong with understandings of care. That is, care-givers are the only authentic carers and people who actually deal with real issues of care. It is at this juncture that she raised the point that educators have sympathy for students, but they do not actually care for them. In relation to Slote's (2007) distinction between empathy and sympathy, I wanted to examine whether caring is inapplicable to education and in particular pedagogical encounters.

Empathy or Sympathy?

Slote (2007: 34–35) distinguishes between empathy and sympathy as follows:

> Thus empathy involves having the feelings of another (involuntarily) aroused in ourselves, as when we see another person in pain. It is as if their pain invades us, and Hume speaks, in this connection, of the contagion between what one person feels and what another comes to feel. However, we can also feel sorry for, bad for, the person who is in pain and positively wish them well. This amounts, as we say, to sympathy for them, and it can happen even if we aren't feeling their pain.

On the one hand, a person has empathy for someone else if such a person comes to feel the other person's pain. In education, a teacher feels the pain of a student when the student does not defend his or her thesis convincingly enough under conditions of intense scrutiny. Perhaps the teacher remembers his or her own pain of not doing too well in an oral examination and thus relates to the pain the student undergoes, as the behaviour of the student clearly arouses the teacher's empathy. On the other hand, a teacher has sympathy for a student who performs poorly in an examination without being him- or herself aroused by the feelings of disappointment experienced by the student. Following Slote (2007: 37–38), Person A only knows the pain of Person B if the latter expresses, exhibits or reflects the pain which he or she internalises. As pronounced by Slote (2007: 38), '[s]o an ethics of empathic caring can say that institutions and laws, as well as social customs and practices, are just if they reflect empathically caring'.

Slote (2007: 107) links the practice of empathic caring to showing respect for someone else. When teachers therefore disrespect students, they do not exhibit empathic caring towards them. I am inclined, then, to hold that respect for individuals can be unpacked in terms of such students. In this way, the autonomy of the student is undermined – that is, disrespecting a student by undermining his or her autonomy is a vindication of a lack of empathic caring. What emphatic caring brings to the practice of teaching is that teachers would be more motivated to support students if they recognise that students' lack of understanding is often associated with the teacher not seeing them as autonomous students who can think for themselves, or as students who lack the capacity to proffer plausible arguments. If this happens, teachers should exercise more empathic caring towards students who require to be uplifted within the pedagogical encounter to the extent that they want to understand things better. Of course, showing respect for students does not mean that a teacher is reluctant to evoke the potentialities of students to come to understanding. Likewise, respect does not mean that a teacher is not prepared to take issue with students when he or she sees that the students are wrong. Instead, respect for students – and, by implication, exercising empathic caring – implies that a teacher will contest what students have to say about this or that, for failing to do so would be to treat students disrespectfully, i.e. without empathic care. In a pedagogical encounter, there is always a need for participants to want to engage, that is, they want to be seen and heard as legitimate participants who have autonomy to shape the encounter. This need on the part of participants requires the willingness of others in the encounter to listen to what they have to say. Put differently, every participant in an encounter yearns to be respected by the other. And, as a way of exhibiting their respect, each participant allows the other to articulate his or her point of view. In this way, participants allow one another to articulate what they have in mind on account of their capability and competence to do so. Of course, showing respect does not mean that everything someone else says should be accepted unconditionally. Quite poignantly, Brian Fay (1996: 239) has the following to say about respect, and I concur:

> Respect demands that we hold others to the intellectual and moral standards we apply to our friends and ourselves. Excusing others from demands of intellectual rigor and honesty or moral sensitivity and wisdom on the grounds that everyone is entitled to his or her opinion no matter how ill-informed or ungrounded, or – worse – on the grounds that others need not or cannot live up to these demands, is to treat them with contempt. We honor others by challenging them when we think they are wrong, and by thoughtfully taking their criticisms of us.

When university teachers show empathic care for their students, they accept students' autonomy to criticise them and, equally, students should be held answerable for making unjustifiable claims. In this way, empathic caring manifests because respect allows participants to engage with 'mutual critical reflection' (Fay, 1996: 240) in pedagogical encounters. This brings me to a discussion of empathic caring in relation to just action. To assume that university teachers cannot really care and that empathic caring is applicable to only the medical profession is to be remiss of what it means to engage respectfully – that is, caringly within an encounter.

Empathic Caring and Justice

In the same way empathic caring involves recognising the pain or vulnerability of someone else, and respecting the autonomy of persons, so an ethic of empathic caring is linked to justice. According to Slote (2007:

167–168), social institutions, practices and customs, as well as political legislation, 'are just if they reflect empathically caring motivation on the part of (enough of) those responsible for originating and maintaining them'. Considering that religious intolerance and persecution, patriarchal social attitudes, and women who do a disproportionate amount of housework, are ways that do not embody empathic caring and, therefore, are unjust (Slote, 2007: 169–171). Similarly, if civil citizens of one country do not show concern for immigrants living outside their own country, they can be said to lack empathic caring.

When teachers and students undermine one another within pedagogical encounters by not allowing each another to speak and justify their points of view, say on this matter or that, they could be said to be lacking empathic caring. Another pertinent example in point is a university curriculum that seems to turn a blind eye to developments about intolerance and injustice pertaining to marginalised peoples. I specifically think of the harassment and intimidation several religious persons have to endure on account of the differences they exhibit in the public domain. If university curricula fail to respond to such pertinent developments in communities, it would not be unfair to associate such curricula with lacking empathic care. The upshot of the afore-mentioned argument is that exercising empathic caring becomes a struggle against religious and racial bigotry, gender oppression and cultural imperialism – in the sense that a specific cultural understanding is considered by some as more superior than that of another community. As Hill (2000: 69) asserts, any person ought to be considered worthy of respect even if such person exhibits value differences of which others may disapprove. Even those blamed for perpetrating religious bigotry in the example mentioned above should be respected as persons, which at least would leave open the door for reconciliation – a matter of practising empathic care. Showing excessive dislike and hatred towards people would undermine the possibility of reconciliation among contending parties. Put differently, empathic care could enhance reconciliation on the basis that without care, human dignity would be undermined and reconciliation might be unlikely. If one does not show empathic care towards others on account of their human dignity it is very unlikely that such persons would in any case be respected and, by implication, co-existing together as humans would be difficult as well.

This brings me to a brief discussion of how empathic care can be cultivated in a university class. Firstly, university curricula should reflect narratives of cultural difference of diverse peoples, say on the African continent. In this way, pedagogical opportunities would be created for students to engage critically with difference and perhaps controversial issues that emanate from race, gender, class and religious differences. Through empathic care, students can learn to appreciate values of others, perhaps unknown to them. Secondly, showing empathic care requires that teachers engage with students about care and justice in relation to trust – that is, through pedagogical intimacy, students and teachers can be afforded opportunities to 'look into each other's eyes and squeeze each other's hands' (Greene, 1994: 25). Thirdly, teachers should initiate students into discussions about constraining injurious speech. That is, students should learn not to use speech to affront other students, although such a constraint does not imply that one has to abandon belligerent discussions with them. Empathic care can reasonably be practised when students learn to constrain harmful speech. In other words, free articulation of thoughts should not be, as Amy Gutmann (2003: 200) puts it, 'an unconstrained licence to discriminate'.

However, my potential critic might legitimately assert that constraining freedom of speech under the guise of practicing empathic care – even if such speech were to be injurious – is tantamount to abruptly curtailing educative practices. Elsewhere (Davids & Waghid, 2019) we have developed the argument that provocative speech cannot be dismissed on account that speech requires of one to engage with thought in any case. In other words, it seems more plausible to reconfigure speech rather than just dismissing it, for the reason that change can only happen when people engage with one another's opposing and at times belligerent views. Yet, in reconfiguring speech, one explicitly recognises the need to counteract harmful and discriminatory speech. For instance, it does not seem convincing merely to expel academics and students from institutions of higher learning when they hold controversial views about societal matters. The point is, they cannot be wished away on the grounds that their views are incommensurate with the dominant views that prevail. Such controversial views, if not dealt with through engagement and rebuttal, will permeate society and might resurface again some other time because the views have not been given sufficient attention. Equally, others might assert that discriminatory and provocative speech does not warrant engagement. Rather, I would posit that engaging with such speech might be a better option in the sense that counter-speech is invariably a more tenable way of dealing with unjust speech than leaving such provocative speech unexamined.

Summary

In this chapter, I have given an account of empathic caring. Such a form of caring manifests in pedagogical encounters in ways teachers and students treat one another with dignity and respect. In addition, I have shown how recognising the pain of others through empathic care can most appropriately be addressed through an understanding of justice when a person constrains him- or herself in speech in pedagogical encounters with others in order to build pedagogical intimacy and trust within university classes.

References

Davids, N., & Waghid, Y. (2019, forthcoming). *Free speech and university encounters: Reconfiguring democratic education.* Rotterdam, The Netherlands: Brill-Sense.

Fay, B. (1996). *Contemporary philosophy of science.* Oxford, UK: Blackwell.

Greene, M. (1994). Teaching for openings: Pedagogy as dialectic. In P. A. Sullivan & D. J. Qually (Eds.), *Pedagogy in the age of politics* (pp. 20–32). Urbana, IL: NCTE.

Gutmann, A. (2003). *Identity in democracy.* Princeton, NJ: Princeton University Press.

Hill, T., Jr. (2000). *Respect, pluralism and justice.* Oxford, UK: Oxford University Press.

Slote, M. (2007). *The ethics of care and empathy.* New York: Routledge.

8

Towards Rhythmic Caring: Cultivating Sceptical Pedagogical Encounters

Introduction

In the previous chapters, I have articulated understandings of caring in relation to inclusion, practicality, authenticity, pragmatism, attentiveness, democracy and empathy. In my view, such understandings of caring can be enacted within pedagogical encounters. However, as I shall argue in this chapter, inasmuch as such moments of attachment come to the fore in encounters, at the same time there can also arise moments of detachment in the encounters on account of scepticism that surface, with reference to Stanley Cavell's (1979) ideas. The rise of scepticism is a real possibility within caring pedagogical encounters. Pursuant to the latter idea, pedagogical encounters might appear to be caringly inclusive, practical, authentic, pragmatic, attentive, democratic and empathic; yet, momentarily, such encounters might also become encounters characterised by moments of non-inclusion, im-practicality, un-authenticity, non-pragmatism, in-attentiveness, non-democracy, and non-empathy. My concern in this chapter is with both the attachment and momentarily detachment from caring. Hence, I am drawn to a notion of rhythmic caring within pedagogical encounters on the grounds that the act of rhythm connects with fluctuations of attachment and detachment or giving and taking. It is not that a particular understanding of caring is abandoned but instead, it is advanced on account of some sceptical lapse that unfolds within pedagogical encounters – a moment of holding back as humans advance to cultivate their relational experience. By way of example, in my doctoral encounters with students, I experience moments when I advance my understandings of particular theoretical views on democratic educational theory. Then, for a while, I hold back my justifications and wait for students to articulate their autonomous ideas on such a theory of education. In this sense, my encounters with students are not relational only, but also characterised by moments of holding back and advancement vis-à-vis theoretical ideas. My encounters with students can therefore be described as rhythmic. In this chapter, I firstly, offer an account of rhythmic caring, and secondly, I show how other notions of caring as elucidated in the previous chapters can be extended to sceptical moments within pedagogical encounters. Concomitantly with the latter, and thirdly, I move on to a discussion of how pedagogical encounters might unfold when rhythmic caring is at play.

Towards an Understanding of Rhythmic Caring

Pursuant to the explication of rhythm I offered in the Preface, and for a further explication of the concept as will be used in relation to caring, I turn in detail to the seminal thoughts of Giorgio Agamben (1994). For Agamben (1994: 98), rhythm is that which causes the work of art to take on the form of 'that which gives every thing its proper station in presence'. More cogently, in his words,

> The word 'rhythm' comes from the Greek ῥέω, to flow, as in the case of water. That which flows does so in a temporal dimension: it flows in time … Yet rhythm – as we commonly understand it – appears to introduce into this eternal flow a split and a stop. Thus in a musical piece, although it is somehow in time, we perceive rhythm as something that escapes the incessant flight of instants and appears almost as the presence of an atemporal dimension in time … There is a stop, and interruption in the incessant

flow of instants that, coming from the future, sinks into the past, and this interruption, this stop, is precisely what gives and reveals the particular status, the mode of presence proper to the work of art or the landscape we have before us. (Agamben, 1994: 99)

I am interested in Agamben's explanation of rhythm as an 'interruption' that comes from the future and sinks into the past. Although the flow of water, as per Agamben's example, is always spontaneous, it can be interrupted only in its presence by recognising that it comes from a future and goes back into a past in some elastic manner. My understanding of rhythm as that which comes from a future and sinks back into a past, is metaphorically used by Agamben to accentuate the presence of rhythm on account of being advanced into the future and held back to return to its past – that is, an occasion of holding back (that is, into a past), and simultaneously opening up into a future. By way of illustration, one can think of an elastic band that is stretched out 'into a future' and then slightly released to make contact with its past through a momentary relation. The elasticity remains in the band so the point of interruption is momentarily or for a while when the band hurls back into the direction of its point of release, but it does not restart again entirely. As aptly, stated by Agamben (1994: 100):

> [R]hythm holds, that is, gives and holds back … Rhythm grants [wo]men both the ecstatic dwelling in a more original dimension and the fall into the flight of measurable time. It holds *epochally* the essence of [wo]man, that is, gives him [her] the gift of being and of nothingness, both of the impulse in the free space of the work and of the impetus toward shadow and ruin. It is the original *ecstasy* that opens for [wo]man the space of his [her] world, and only by starting from it can he [she] experience freedom and alienation …

Based on the aforementioned account of rhythm, I infer that rhythm is a moment of interruption in the presence of a person's work on account of which he or she endeavours to open up to what is still to come and simultaneously resists (holds back) by going back into the past. Put in a different way, rhythmic action can be an advancing movement of sudden interruption coupled with a temporary suspension to hold the action in the present. It can be associated with hurling one's emotion into the open and simultaneously holding it back towards a past. In other words, when a person experiences his or her 'being-in-the-world' as a condition of presence, a world opens up of 'willed and free activity' (Agamben, 1994: 100), which he or she attains in relation to a past and future. Rhythmic action in relation to caring, therefore, implies that such a human emotion ventures into a future towards a care receiver, but simultaneously, an emotive interruption unfolds, that holds back the care-giver from releasing his or her care freely in order for the care receiver to encounter a moment of ecstasy or pleasure in his or her own presence. The point of rhythmic caring is that caring, firstly, happens *with* others. That is, caring in rhythm is not done for someone. Instead, it is initiated by someone to which others respond. Secondly, the initiation of care is not entirely unidirectional as if caring is done for or about doing this or that for another or other persons. Consequently, when caring is done *with* others, people remain in the present, yet are free and included. Much like a student who ventures imaginatively into a future in the quest to understand a theoretical idea, so the student's imagination is somewhat retarded in order not to lose sight of his or her previous understandings that actually propelled his or her imagination into the unexpected he or she is about to encounter. It is a matter of remaining in touch, yet fully cognisant of his or her imagination to see things differently and to encounter yet what is not known to him or her. This brings me to a discussion of rhythmic care in relation to looking sceptically at the notions of care espoused in the previous chapters.

Scepticism and Rhythmic Care Within Pedagogical Encounters

Stanley Cavell (1979: 440) brings into question the idea that one can completely know another person. One might know a person's name or his or her residential address or marital status, yet, following Cavell (1979: 440), such knowledge is not sufficient to know a person. In other words, there might be 'best cases' for knowing a person – such as those mentioned above – but one would be quite disappointed in one's knowing of others because there might be some things which one does not know or which one may never come to know. As soon as one comes to know that others will invariably be imperfectly known to you, it would not be inappropriate to attribute one's doubt in completely knowing others on account of them (the others) being strangers to you (Cavell, 1979: 443). The point is, all that one can know about others is what others are able to show you of themselves (Cavell, 1979: 443). For example, I would not know the disappointment of a student unless he or she shows me how disappointed he or she is. But even then, one cannot completely or perfectly know others as you would be disappointed to know what you do not know of others or what others do not know of you. Considering that in human relations among oneself and others, you and others can never be perfectly known; there will always be room for doubt, disappointment and suspicion about your knowledge of others and, equally, others' knowledge of you. On the grounds that one's knowledge of others can be only partial and by implication prejudicial, you cannot avoid being suspicious about your knowledge of others. And, as Cavell (1979: 441) posits, an appropriate way of knowing others can be only in relation to 'one's experience of others'. You and others cannot entirely ever know one another. It is such a suspicion that raises one's scepticism in the sense that your ignorance of others on the basis of knowing them only partially through experience, is lived out in respect of your relationships with them. In other words, one and others can never completely know one another and, what they come to know is as a consequence of what has been shown to them by others. In a way, knowing others can happen only through some practice of scepticism whereby one is aware of the limitations in knowing another completely. It is such a Cavellian understanding of scepticism that can affect the way humans care for others. My view is that scepticism resonates with an enactment of rhythmic care because caring *with* others by necessity requires that others be only partially or imperfectly known to one another. The point I am making, is that one does not have to be known perfectly in order for care to manifest. One might be partially known to others, yet care could manifest.

In the section below, I justify the latter in relation to the exercise of rhythmic care within pedagogical encounters.

When teachers, firstly, treat their relationships with students as a sceptical encounter, they acknowledge that they would not be able to know their students completely. They (the teachers) would then have to commit themselves to experiencing students. That is, experiencing who students are, and realising that what students bring to encounters are different from simply knowing them. On the grounds of what students present to teachers, teachers act in a manner whereby they project, say, empathic care within the encounter. In doing so, teachers accept the possibility that they will never completely know the vulnerability of students, and they will act only on account of what they experience with the students. In raising their suspicion (and scepticism) within encounters, teachers therefore advance their empathic care with the understanding to interrupt their projection on the grounds that students will present their arguments or views more convincingly. Momentarily, with the insertion of radical doubt within the encounter, a teacher suspends his or her premature judgement of students' views to allow the free flow of thoughts to ensue. Furthermore, a teacher in his or her presence acts non-empathically on the grounds of not showing, at least momentarily, much empathy within the encounter. This interruption with suspicion is not an abandonment of the students, but rather an instantaneous opening where students commit themselves in earnest to see things for themselves independent of the care of a teacher or at least, dependent on the momentary interruption of the teacher's care. In this way, scepticism seems to enhance the exercise of rhythmic care within pedagogical encounters. The encounter is rhythmic because in its continuous unfolding, it is momentarily interrupted by an act of non-empathy, after which, empathy again ensues.

In addition, engaging with scepticism within pedagogical encounters also brings to the surface other dimensions of human interconnectedness vis-à-vis a notion of rhythmic care. Firstly, while engaging sceptically with students in a pedagogical encounter, in a Cavellian sense (1979: 438), the teacher becomes a mirror image of the other, which in turn, makes a teacher answerable to students and students answerable to a teacher. This answerability to one another is in tune with a notion of attentive care. Yet, when a teacher exhibits his or her answerability to students he or she also momentarily interrupts his or her action to allow the student to recognise the inattentiveness that should spur him or her invariably on to make sense of matters for him- or herself. Momentarily, such a disruptive pedagogical encounter also lends itself to being non-democratic in the sense that the union between the teacher and his or her students had been halted instantaneously for the sake of stimulating more autonomous learning on the part of students.

Secondly, treating one's relationship with others as a sceptical encounter implies that one has to acknowledge others as humans and, at the same time, others must acknowledge one as being human. This is so since humans have the potential to treat one another with scepticism. As remarked by Cavell (1979: 433), 'I have to acknowledge humanity in the other, and the basis of it seems to lie in me.' It is only through recognising one another's humanity that teachers and students can engage in sceptical pedagogical encounters. In an encounter, a teacher therefore ought to acknowledge his or her students as equally human, and therefore merit to be treated as co-humans in a transaction. However, raising doubts about the transactional relationship could result in a momentary interruption that would render the encounter non-transactional. Such a situation, in turn, would have the effect that students and teachers become more attuned to the encounter in order for teaching and learning to ensue. Unless, of course, teachers and students do not wish to remain bounded by the encounter, in which case the situation would be tantamount to mis-acknowledging one another's presence. The implication is that the possibility will be enhanced for the encounter to yield, perhaps, more desirable results, such as improved teaching and learning. Sometimes in university classes, teaching becomes too tedious and cumbersome, and encounters require some sort of awakening that would stimulate teachers and students to act anew with more enthusiasm and vigour. Such a ruptured moment would lead to better recognition of one another and, by implication, perhaps to more rigorous pedagogical encounters. And, if such a ruptured instance were to ensue, pedagogical encounters ought to be subjected to scepticism as such a notion of distrust would enhance the possibility for rhythmic caring to manifest within pedagogical encounters.

Thirdly, following Cavell's (1979: 269) account of scepticism, it seems as if moments of attachment and detachment and acknowledgement and avoidance are emphasised. In his words:

> It provides a door through which someone alienated can return by offering of and the acceptance of explanation, excuses and justifications, or by the respect one human being will show another who sees and accepts the responsibility for a position which he himself would not adopt. (Cavell, 1979: 269)

Within pedagogical encounters, it is quite possible for teachers to become detached from students momentarily, yet remaining attached on account of the sceptical form the encounter takes. For instance, teachers can provoke students to speak their minds, yet, they (the teachers) can for a while just be detached from students with the understanding that in that moment, students' potentialities would be evoked to come to perhaps a better understanding about a curriculum matter. Similarly, it is possible for students to become excluded from encounters with the view that they will return by providing their justifications for a temporary exclusion. In this way, through the ruptured moment of scepticism, pedagogical encounters can become non-inclusive and simultaneously remain attached to such encounters. What follows is that rhythmic caring would manifest as students remain included and present, yet for a while, un-included – yet not entirely or permanently excluded from the encounter. That is, the possibility remains for students to experience inclusion, despite challenges being posed to their inclusion. And, when such students remain included, the possibility is always there for them to act authentically, for instance in relation to critical reflection about their work. The possibility that they remain un-included depends at least on an understanding that inclusion is possible. In other words, non-inclusion is different from exclusion as the possibility that one remains included is always there except that such a possibility is momentarily thwarted. Yet, permanent exclusion does not ensue. However, when students remain un-included for a while on account of a ruptured moment, they might be spurred on to think more authentically about a curriculum matter and, by implication, remain included within pedagogical encounters. In this way, it seems possible for students to be cared for rhythmically within a pedagogical encounter on the grounds that such a form of caring allows for inclusion and non-inclusion to happen without exclusive or complete abandonment of the other.

I specifically think of my own teaching of philosophical concepts to post-graduate teacher education students. Many of these students enter my classroom without any basic understanding of philosophy. They are introduced to concepts in relation to which they ought to make connections with their practical experiences during pre-service teacher education sessions. I often hear students complain about what they perceive to be a lack of relevance of concepts such as *phronesis* (practical reasoning) and *praxis* (doing action). I then urge them to think through the concepts and attempt to make connections with that which makes sense to them in relation to the subjects they teach. When they make sense of the concepts they have to consider themselves as being included within a pedagogical encounter. However, when they do not make sense of a concept and fail to connect such a concept to an experience of learning, they should consider themselves as momentarily un-included in an encounter. And, when they perhaps make sense of a concept in relation to a learning experience after a while or having been exposed to deliberations about the concept in class, they could rescind their position of non-inclusion if they were to have developed some better understanding of a concept. The point is, within pedagogical encounters, students should not necessarily be subjected to a permanent exclusion, for that in itself would mark the end of learning. However, if they were to be subjected to a momentary non-inclusion, the possibility is always there that they might come to understand through their own or other's explications of concepts. When they are included they are cared for; however, when they are un-included they might not be cared for momentarily. Care therefore takes on a form of provoking understanding and for a while within an encounter, they pursue their thoughts, and care on the part of a teacher is momentarily withheld. Care is therefore given and simultaneously withdrawn – that is when care becomes rhythmic.

Summary

In this chapter, I have made an argument for rhythmic caring within pedagogical encounters. Such a notion of caring has the potential to interrupt encounters on the basis of scepticism. Scepticism influences pedagogical encounters in such a way that teachers and students acknowledge one another's humanity and, in turn, they develop a capacity to hold back on judgements to allow deliberations to ensue spontaneously. Within such pedagogical encounters, a momentary act of rupturing hold teachers and students back to reassert themselves within encounters in order for thoughts to be rendered more justifiably. The point is, students encounter moments of inclusion and non-inclusion without the possibility that they will be subjected to a permanent exclusion from pedagogical encounters. If the latter happens, the possibility for learning and teaching, for that matter, will always be there. This brings me to the next chapter, in which I consider a notion of cosmopolitan caring.

References

Agamben, G. (1994). *The man without content* (G. Albert, Trans.). Stanford, CA: Stanford University Press.

Cavell, S. (1979). *The claim of reason: Wittgenstein, skepticism, morality, and tragedy*. Oxford, UK: Oxford University Press.

9

Cosmopolitan Caring: On Reflexive Loyalty to the Known and Reflexive Openness to the New

Introduction

In the previous chapter, I developed a notion of rhythmic caring, which holds the potential to interrupt pedagogical encounters in such a way that the potentialities of teachers and students are evoked to come up with new and unforeseen possibilities within pedagogical encounters. As has been alluded to in the previous chapters, caring is not just a virtue that is practiced by humans in relation to other humans. Caring can also be linked to other acts of virtue that could contribute to harnessing a good society, most notably, empathy and cosmopolitanism. In this chapter, I consider the relationship between cosmopolitanism and caring and, in turn, proffer a defence of rhythmic caring. I argue that cosmopolitan caring is an instance of rhythmic caring, which holds the possibility for pedagogical encounters to become more enriching – that is, being reflexively loyal to what is known, and exhibiting a reflexive openness to what is still to come.

Caring as Cosmopolitans Within Pedagogical Encounters

My pedagogical encounters with several students from other African countries have taken on a challenging dimension over the last decade. Many students felt comfortable to share their pedagogical challenges with me, such as their difficulty in coming to understand philosophical concepts. I would be the first to acknowledge that the Anglo-Saxon tradition of doing philosophy of education has been dominant in my teaching. However, as I was challenged by the epistemological hindrances many African students experience within our pedagogical encounters, I had to rely mainly on elucidations of philosophical concepts through the lenses of prominent African thinkers. Some of my African students therefore found it extremely appealing and relevant when I invoked understandings of major African thinkers in and about philosophy of education. As has been mentioned previously in this book, although my own initiation into the Anglo-Saxon tradition of philosophy of education should not be discounted, I felt quite at home in engaging with thoughts about philosophy of education as seen through the eyes of prominent African thinkers, including those from the diaspora. And, it is not surprising that some of my African students and I produced a book entitled *African democratic citizenship education revisited* (Waghid & Davids, 2018) as a manifestation of our deliberative work on African philosophy of education. In this book, an important aspect of philosophy of education emerged: philosophy of education of relevance to Africa is a distinctive theory of education that has practical implications for major problems on the continent. Two aspects emerged from my engagement with African students in and about philosophy of education. Firstly, African philosophy of education is real with a distinctive theory of understanding – i.e. all human action is constituted by a notion of equality. In other words, all humans – including Africans – have something equal to say about the advancement of the human condition. Secondly, all humans have a capacity to act with justice. The point about our work on African democratic citizenship education is that, irrespective of the continent on which Africans are situated, they have the capacity to act in the interest of a common humanity and to do so with justice. What follows, from my work with African students, is that a concern for the other and its otherness should be considered an enabling condition for any plausible understanding of philosophy of education. Based on such a view, it is, therefore, not unusual to talk about caring for the other in its otherness. Put differently, it is not unjustifiable to start talking about the notion of cosmopolitan caring considering that such a form of caring is inextricably linked to the position of the other and its otherness. Consequently, in the book mentioned above, we specifically look at notions of caring with others in their respective countries on the continent. Next, I reflect on what cosmopolitan caring entails.

According to David Hansen (2011: xiii), cosmopolitanism is an ancient concept 'that evokes images of moral solidarity with people the world over'. Unlike universalism, cosmopolitanism signifies a 'human capacity to be open reflectively to the larger world, while remaining loyal reflectively to local concerns, commitments, and values' (Hansen, 2011: xiii). More distinctly, cosmopolitanism holds out the prospect of a life in which people learn to balance a reflective openness to that which is still to come with a reflective loyalty to the known (Hansen, 2011: 1). A cosmopolitan-minded person therefore assists people 'in moving closer and closer *apart* and further and further *together*' (Hansen, 2011: 3). In moving closer and closer apart, the possibility is always there that people living at a distance from one another can be held together by an attentive care for one another and, being further and further together implies that people who do not live in close proximity can find themselves in solidarity on the grounds of an empathic moral cause. In such a way, the notion of cosmopolitanism seems to be in harmony with multiple instances of caring – that is, attentive and empathic caring. Yet, considering that such forms of care make people attentive to one another on account of their differences and commonalities and make the possibility of empathy among them fairly real, it would not be unreasonable to talk about a notion of cosmopolitan caring. Cosmopolitan caring seems to emanate from both attentive and empathic human concerns. Yet, being attentive to one another raises the possibility that people are apart (different) on account of their closeness to one another. Similarly, people can be in solidarity, yet not necessarily in close proximity to one another. The point I am making on account of the afore-mentioned notion of cosmopolitanism, is that people are apart and in solidarity on the basis of who they are, including their commonalities and differences. Their differences are a vindication of their otherness and, hence, people of difference are in a cosmopolitan relationship with each another. It is such a notion of cosmopolitan togetherness and difference that has some bearing on the relationships of care among them.

Considering that cosmopolitanism is conceptually linked to a reflexive loyalty to the known and a reflexive openness to what is still to come, it can be deduced that a notion of cosmopolitan caring is, therefore, an act of being reflectively loyal to the local (known) and reflectively open to what is not yet (Hansen, 2011: 18). Such an understanding of cosmopolitan caring privileges the practice of justice towards others, which includes acting humanely toward others and their otherness. And, when people embark on cosmopolitan caring, they recognise the importance of avoiding doing harm to others, i.e. practicing humanity towards all others (Hansen, 2011: 55). The upshot of such a view of caring is that people would not refuse to interact with ideas from culturally diverse groups, and they would also not act in a judgemental and dismissive way towards those considered as different (Hansen, 2011: 70). The implication is that cosmopolitan caring accentuates a pragmatic attentiveness to human vulnerability, violence, environmental degradation and economic shocks that reverberate around the globe (Hansen, 2011: 73). Not surprisingly, cosmopolitan caring can cultivate human solidarities in a world marked by injustice, war and persistent uncertainty (Hansen, 2011: 74).

Moreover, in relation to pedagogical encounters, cosmopolitan caring would make students more attentive to learning from others because it is a process 'that brings the person into the world and the world into the person, and that indirectly positions him or her to contribute to larger communities' (Hansen, 2011: 86). If the latter occurs, communities and individuals are in a process of becoming 'through the experience of reflective openness to the new fused with reflective loyalty to the known' (Hansen, 2011: 86). And, within pedagogical encounters, teachers and students reflectively open to the new and reflectively loyal to the known would conduct their deliberations 'at the intersection of the strange and familiar, the surprising and the expected' (Hansen, 2011: 86). By implication, through cosmopolitan caring, teachers and students would be prompted not just to talk with one another, listen to the views of one another, but also to talk back to one another. As aptly stated by Hansen (2011: 89), cosmopolitan caring –

> [M]eans participating in pluralist change as an agent, as an actor, rather than remaining passive or merely reactive to events ... cosmopolitan [caring] is not something that happens to people, it is something that people do ... They think about their setting and the world writ large. And the porosity to the environments in which they move differs from that of certain rocks in which water merely passes through.

This brings me to a discussion of some of the implications of cosmopolitan caring for pedagogical encounters. Firstly, cosmopolitan carers aspire to work together, which means that teachers and students engage in pedagogical encounters because of a commitment to work together. This implies that both see the need to be influenced by one another's thoughts. In a way, their caring for one another works in a supportive way as they recognise that they can learn from one another – that is, they appreciate 'what it means to dwell educationally' (Hansen, 2011: 117). Many of the African students in my philosophy class are in agreement that an initiation into a discourse of African philosophy of education requires of students and me to be open to learning from and with one another. It is not sufficient that I explicate some of the views of prominent African thinkers on education. Rather, students recognise their autonomy to act willingly in the pursuit of conjuring up ideas and elucidations of such a philosophy of education. Secondly, considering that a core value of cosmopolitan caring is to show 'a reflective openness to the new and reflective loyalty to the known' (Hansen, 2011: 113), pedagogical encounters would be conceived as pedagogical openings for both teachers and students. In other words, in such encounters, there would always arise the possibility to see new imaginings. Teachers and students would, in the words of Hansen (2011: 118), 'constitute an already existing cosmopolitan community ... [with] an abiding disposition to share ideas, methods, and philosophies across any number of cultural markers'. Here, I specifically think of a notion of an African philosophy of education that aims to examine major problems on the continent of Africa, and then to examine the implications of such an analysis for higher education in particular. The point is, such a view of philosophy of education could not have emanated from my own thoughts without also having considered the views articulated by my students. Again, in reference to a massive open online course (MOOC) on Teaching for Change, in which we examine at length in the book *Rupturing African philosophy of teaching and learning: Ubuntu justice and education* (Waghid, Waghid, & Waghid, 2018), a notion of African philosophy of education as an explication of major problems with the aim to examine educational implications for higher learning, would not have been possible without the analytical and at times descriptive contributions of my students.

Thirdly, cosmopolitan caring stimulates teachers to recognise the enormous cognitive powers of students and, without coercing students to do things, they nominate themselves as change agents 'while not ignoring the genuine service that meaningful [teacher] support can provide them [students]' (Hansen, 2011: 124). My interest is in the cosmopolitan concern of becoming a change agent. When teachers and students commit themselves to becoming change agents they are at once concerned about the importance of the curriculum to affect their education. The point is, teachers and students who are cosmopolitan carers set out for themselves to cultivate a world that is just and in which human relations are nurtured for the betterment of all. The implication is that teachers and students would not just talk about change but would actually do something about making change happen. Of course, this does not mean that one first requires some utopian understanding of a just world before you embark on action to change the wrongs in the world. Rather, instead of just paying lip service to justice in this world, humans embark on initiatives that would enhance human prosperity. This would invariably require that people commit themselves to speaking out against global injustices, wars, global warming and deforestation, economic insecurity and human trafficking. In short, teachers and students as cosmopolitan carers would remain open and loyal *within* pedagogical encounters to bring about a change to the injustices that characterise our world today.

Finally, the question arises: why is cosmopolitan caring an instance of rhythmic caring? When teachers and students – as cosmopolitan carers – are deliberatively engaged in pedagogical encounters, they also create openings where the familiar or established interrupts the strange or not so familiar. Teachers and students are both driven by what is expected of them and by what they can accomplish together. Yet, they are also interrupted by moments of surprise where the not so familiar unfolds within their encounters. Consequently, as teachers and students, they fluctuate between what is and what is yet to come on account of their cosmopolitan caring actions. In this way, their actions assume the form of rhythmic caring as they listen, engage and also become open to the unexpected and the incalculable within the encounters. As Maxine Greene (1995: 19) so eloquently reminds us, 'the role of imagination [and I would include cosmopolitan caring as well] is not to resolve, not to point the way, not to improve. It is to awaken, to disclose the ordinarily unseen, unheard, and unexpected'. The point is, cosmopolitan caring allows students and teachers to be attentive to one another as they endeavour to confront the intellectually surprised or unexpected. They are momentarily in a relationship of empathic care in terms of which they are provoked to come to their own ways of seeing the world as they engage with difference and otherness. In a rhythmic way, teachers and students encounter one another with evocation and surprise, provocation and interruption as they collectively make sense of their learning. As cosmopolitans in a caring relationship, they are destined to come to know without abandoning that which they already know. Instead, they become reflexively loyal to what they know, and simultaneously reflexively open to what is still to come in a relationship constituted by rhythmic care.

Summary

In this chapter, I made an argument in defence of cosmopolitan caring as an instance of rhythmic caring. Through cosmopolitan caring, teachers and students are able to remain loyal and reflective to what is known to them, as well as to work together within pedagogical encounters and to remain open and reflective to what is in becoming. Because they are both stimulated to remain reflectively loyal to what is known and reflectively open to the new, it seems as if pedagogical encounters vis-à-vis the presence of cosmopolitanism are commensurate with rhythmic caring. In this way, there is always the possibility that things might be seen otherwise. Next, I discuss the African ethic of *ubuntu* in relation to caring.

References

Greene, M. (1995). *Releasing the imagination: Essays on education, the arts, and social change*. San Francisco: Jossey-Bass.

Hansen, D. T. (2011). *The teacher and the world: A study of cosmopolitanism as education*. London: Routledge.

Waghid, Y., & Davids, N. (Eds.). (2018). *African democratic citizenship education revisited*. New York: Palgrave Macmillan.

Waghid, Y., Waghid, F., & Waghid, Z. (2018). *Rupturing African teaching and learning: Ubuntu justice and education*. New York: Palgrave Macmillan.

10

Ubuntu Caring: Cultivating Moral, Compassionate, and Restorative Justice in University Education

Introduction

In the previous chapter, I referred to some pedagogical encounters with African students from the continent. I also referred to some of my latest thoughts on African teaching and learning and how rupturing could manifest in pedagogical encounters. In many ways, the human self is invariably engaged with others in encounters and, together, they shape such encounters. Yet, like most encounters, pedagogical encounters are not without a purpose – that is, encounters have some kind of worthwhile intent that is worked towards. It is my understanding that human encounters on the African continent cannot be devoid of achieving a sense of humanness and interconnectedness among people. In this way, it seems as if encounters have an *ubuntu* orientation on the grounds that the latter is connected to the cultivation of acts of human interdependence and dignity. My contention in this chapter is linked to the idea of *ubuntu* being connected to caring, as caring cannot occur with recognising the engagement of the self with others on the basis of mutual respect. In this chapter, I develop the concept of *ubuntu* as an instance of rhythmic caring. Consequently, I firstly, make an argument why the African ethic of *ubuntu* is coupled with caring. Secondly, I show how *ubuntu* caring emanates from a recent work on cultivating African teaching and learning to which I referred in the previous chapter (see Waghid & Davids, 2018). And, thirdly, I offer an account of *ubuntu* caring in order to show how teaching and learning in an African university could become educationally more defensible.

On the Notion of *Ubuntu* Caring

At the time of writing this chapter, we had just completed a book, entitled *Rupturing African teaching and learning: Ubuntu justice and education* (Waghid, Waghid, & Waghid, 2018) in which we argue for a notion of *ubuntu* justice as a constitutive feature of university education. Implicit in our defence of *ubuntu* caring, there is an interconnectedness with humane virtues of morality, compassion and restoration right from the start. *Ubuntu* justice is an ethic of care that constitutes at least three dimensions of caring: moral respect towards one another; concern for the vulnerabilities of all; and the prevention, eradication and cultivation of human interdependence (Waghid et al., 2018: 48). Firstly, showing moral respect to all, including those we might strongly resent, is an *ubuntu* practice whereby the recognition and acknowledgement of others are always prioritised. Dismissing people on the basis of cultural, political and ethnic differences would be an act of remission in the sense that no one can or should wish other humans away, or consider others as unworthy of being engaged with. An *ubuntu* ethic of care prioritises the recognition that all are equal and that no person can or should ever undermine or disrespect someone else's right of belonging to humanity. Of course, my potential critic might rightfully assert that in many parts of Africa, antagonism, violent hostility, and war crimes are committed against humanity, and my critic might therefore see no reason why *ubuntu* would work anywhere else on the continent. *Ubuntu* caring is not an instant panacea to resolve inhumanity and gross violations of human rights on the continent. Rather, *ubuntu* caring is an ethic of care that offers opportunities to resolve human conflict. That is, the potential is always there, but to assume that disrespect and inhumanity will all of a sudden dissipate is asking too much of *ubuntu* caring itself. If such an ethic is practiced, the potential is always there for viable change to occur. Furthermore, through *ubuntu* caring, the potential is always there for human beings to treat one another with dignity and respect and to aspire towards moral actions, such as humanness and non-violence. Within pedagogical encounters, teachers and students acting in accordance with an *ubuntu* ethic of care first of all announce one another's right to engage in deliberation, and come up with points of view that might not be acceptable to all – that is, through *ubuntu* caring, interdependence among teachers and students is always accentuated irrespective of how diverse, provocative and uncomfortable deliberations might turn out to be. Through an ethic of *ubuntu* care, there is always the possibility for teachers and students to engage in belligerent and distressful encounters. Yet, they remain deliberatively engaged on account of *ubuntu* caring towards others in moments of profound provocation that cannot simply be wished away.

Secondly, an *ubuntu* ethic of care makes it possible for humans to consider always not causing injury or harm to all others. In pedagogical encounters, teachers and students would therefore not embark on dismissing or undermining the integrity and self-worth of one another. If the latter happens, such encounters would be remiss of an *ubuntu* ethic of care. By implication, the use of abusive and contemptuous expressions can never be considered appropriate under the guise of unconstrained freedom of speech within encounters. *Ubuntu* caring holds the potential for teachers and students to be held accountable for remaining in the deliberations as long as rude and obnoxious speech does not find its way into the encounters. It is here that *ubuntu* caring affords participants the right to withdraw from deliberations as violent behaviour and attitudes do not find any justifiable spaces within pedagogical encounters. As soon as violence enters any deliberation, speech in itself has been aborted and there is no reason for any deliberation to continue on account of the presence of detestable or horrible speech.

Thirdly, central to the notion of *ubuntu* caring, is the idea that humans ought to work towards equality, compassion and reconciliation (Waghid et al., 2018: 48). When people treat one another equally, they do so on the grounds that they recognise one another's equal intelligence to speak and disrupt the conversations. Likewise, when humans have compassion for one another, they recognise the vulnerabilities of others, and through an attentiveness to reconcile with others they endeavour to do the unexpected momentarily (as in rhythmic care), for instance, to do the unexpected by offering forgiveness. If there is no forgiveness, there will not be an opportunity to advance deliberative encounters. What holds people back from engaging continuously in deliberative encounters is the unwillingness of others to reconcile through forgiveness. I am not using forgiveness in a theological sense. Rather, I consider forgiving someone as a temporary adjustment in one's feelings of resentment towards another one seemingly dislikes, in order for the conversation to remain ongoing towards what is not yet known. In relation to pedagogical encounters, exercising forgiveness as an instance of *ubuntu* care would possibly hold teachers and students together in the deliberations. What an act of reconciliation then does, is to afford teachers and students the recognition that they can make mistakes in their judgements. Yet, the possibility remains that they can be shown otherwise and through pedagogical forgiveness come to see the point, perhaps, differently too. But for the latter to unfold, pedagogical encounters ought to draw on *ubuntu* caring in order that the possibility will always remain there for reconciliation to occur even if viewpoints had been considered as strongly incommensurable. The point is, *ubuntu* caring encourages teachers and students to take risks because without risk taking within pedagogical encounters the possibility might not be there to see things differently or anew. Elsewhere, I have articulated a notion of *ubuntu*, similar to the one of *ubuntu* care I am now articulating. It is worth to consider it here again:

> *Ubuntu* [care] or human interdependence and connectedness can effect hospitable and hostile encounters that are both respectful and compassionate. Such encounters make humans what they are on the basis that their educatedness and hence their humanity would impact the way they acknowledge one another, provoke one another to see things differently and stimulate one another to act with responsibility. (Waghid, 2018: 61)

Ubuntu caring as an act of hospitality implies that people would welcome one another within encounters on the basis of being human. Despite their similarities and differences, humans remain willing to engage with one another within encounters on the basis that there is always an inherent expectation that as long as encounters last, there is always the possibility that people would see things anew. Likewise, *ubuntu* as an act of hostility does not rule out disagreements among people. Through disagreements, people would remain favourably positioned to take risks on account that they are prepared to take risks in the light of the possibility that they do not have to see things in a similar way. This brings me to a discussion of *ubuntu* care in relation to the idea of a decolonised African university. I tackle this issue on the grounds that decoloniality seems to be a way in which universities on the African continent endeavour to reconstruct and reimagine alternative possibilities that will bring the institutions and their peoples in hospitable and hostile encounters.

Decoloniality, an African University and *Ubuntu* Care

Universities in Africa have been under threat since the days of colonialism and post-colonialism on the grounds that autonomous thinking, academic freedom and engaged scholarship have been seriously hampered, and the quest for institutions that could serve the public good has been dealt a serious blow. One of the primary reasons why universities on the continent have been constantly retarded in their urgency to move beyond the strangleholds of colonialism and post-colonialism is a consequence of the curtailment of democratic citizenship education to manifest at institutions of higher learning. As we articulated in a recent book (Waghid & Davids, 2018: ix),

> [A]t a political level, it did not behove colonised nation-states to act according to values of democracy and citizenship primarily because of repression, exploitation and exclusion. Of course, this does not mean that Africa's peoples did not resist their political exclusion and by implication announced their democratic and citizenship aspirations. However, such often-prohibited demands were easily quelled by the coercive powers of the colonial authorities. Likewise, many indigenous communities by and large succumb to their own political dictatorships that mostly served as political proxies to procure colonial rule.

The point is, universities on the African continent did not escape the colonial and post-colonial barrage of unauthentic claims about African society. Of course, against such a background of political subjugation, African communities evolved in opposition to the political malaise. Unfortunately, African societies could not entirely evade the lack of democratic citizenship education that prevailed, and universities on the continent have subsequently been used to quell autonomous, deliberative and emancipatory scholarship. As I have argued elsewhere, if African universities were to enhance their claims to imaginative and flagship status, teaching and learning practices ought to be buttressed by the emancipatory concerns of freedom, autonomy, openness, criticality and deliberation (Waghid et al., 2018: 163). And, for the latter to happen, African communities ought to become far more attuned to the underlying meanings of democratic citizenship education. It is with regard to the latter that *ubuntu* care could play a decolonised role.

In my view, *ubuntu* care requires that people engage openly with one another as they endeavour to come to terms with one another's cultural, political, socio-economic and ethnic concerns. When they do so, it is presumed that their predispositions and caring actions manifest in active participatory communal engagement. In other words, university teachers and students become prepared to act as publicly informed citizens capable of engaging with complex local and global concerns (Waghid et al., 2018: 162). Considering that *ubuntu* care is an emancipatory, humanising and politico-pedagogical act, the possibility is always there to counteract injustices such as genocide, human trafficking, ethnic conflict and wars of terror (Achebe, 1989: 85). If this happens, the possibility that decoloniality would manifest in African societies, is highly likely. This is so on account that *ubuntu* care creates spaces for marginalised communities to rehumanise African societies (Waghid et al., 2018: 162). It is *ubuntu* care that stimulates universities' teachers and students on the African continent 'to work towards decoloniality in the quest to undermine racism, exclusion, humiliation, deforestation and other forms of human and non-human injustice' (Waghid et al., 2018: 163). *Ubuntu* care has the potential to assist teachers and students to confront and depose injustice, humiliation and exclusion – a matter of cultivating decoloniality.

In the main, decoloniality is an attempt not only to break away from the constraining and debilitating effects of authoritarian rule, but most poignantly also to inculcate into the peoples of Africa that they have an autonomous voice which has the potential to take into controversy whatever hampers societal development and emancipatory human action. That is, decoloniality is primarily concerned with the cultivation of just and equal human relationships where people deliberate about matters that concern their advancement and where the quest for peaceful co-existence becomes a societal priority. Equally, decoloniality is concerned with an advancement of humans' sense of being and belonging where the possibility of exclusion can be derailed. It is coloniality that hinders human progress as peoples remain subjected to the hegemony of others and where the possibility of exercising their freedoms and emancipatory concerns is severely curtailed. If decoloniality could manifest in human practices, it seems rather unlikely that their actions for justice and humanness would be unjustifiably jeopardised. One way to take care of the unbearable effects of decoloniality in our educational institutions is to invoke a notion of *ubuntu* caring.

Summary

Ubuntu caring creates opportunities for teachers and students to engage respectfully and dignifiedly with one another. When people respect one another, they are encouraged to engage with one another in terms of which their human freedoms can be enacted. Showing a sense of dignity towards the existence and points of view of others is a matter of creating conditions where humans remain inclined towards the cultivation of peaceful living. Pedagogical encounters constituted by *ubuntu* care could evolve into imaginative openings and reopenings where university teachers and students can favourably think of rehumanising society as injustices and enslavement of whatever kind will be counteracted in emancipatory fashion. It is at the interface of deliberative encounters and a critical reflection about conditions that hamper human flourishing that decoloniality can arise as a way to advance African universities' intellectual sojourns. I cannot imagine an African university not being attuned to deliberative inquiry, the recognition of autonomous intellectual pursuits, and an ongoing struggle against societal injustice, if such decoloniality were to be internalised by both teachers and students.

References

Achebe, C. (1989). *Hopes and impediments: Selected essays*. New York: Anchor Books.

Waghid, Y. (2018). On the educational potential of ubuntu. In E. J. Takyi-Amoako & N. T. Assié-Lumumba (Eds.), *Re-visioning education in Africa: Ubuntu-inspired education for humanity* (pp. 55–66). New York: Palgrave Macmillan.

Waghid, Y., & Davids, N. (Eds.). (2018). *African democratic citizenship education revisited*. New York: Palgrave Macmillan.

Waghid, Y., Waghid, F., & Waghid, Z. (2018). *Rupturing African teaching and learning: Ubuntu justice and education*. New York: Palgrave Macmillan.

11

A Reflective Account on Dimensions of Caring: Moments of Care Within Journal Editorship, Doctoral Supervision, and Deanship

Introduction

Considering that the elucidations on care in the previous chapters invariably involved my articulations in and about educational encounters within an HE context, I thought it apposite to produce a chapter on my own reflections about my collective roles as journal editor, supervisor and dean of a faculty of education during more than two decades in higher education. What I hope to show in this chapter, is that some of the notions of caring – especially democratic, cosmopolitan and *ubuntu* caring as instances of rhythmic caring – espoused throughout this book, have not been alien to my academic involvement for many years in a university setting. I will endeavour to link some of the dimensions of caring that I have accounted for in this book to my engagement with editorship, student supervision and deanship in a university setting. In this way, I envisage to contextualise some of the aspects of caring in relation to my personal, public and professional sojourn as a philosopher of education.

Care and Journal Editorship

When I became editor-in-chief of the *South African Journal of Higher Education (SAJHE)* more than fifteen years ago, I did not realise that I would be occupying a very prestigious and demanding position in academe. The latter is so, in the light of South African universities' reliance on state funding for their publications in what is known as recognised 'accredited journals'. The *SAJHE* is recognised as one of South Africa's top academic journals, and in Africa, it is rated among the fifty most significant journals out of a total of more than 1400 journals considered accredited. A journal editor has to consider every article in conjunction with reviews of peers as publishable or not in the journal. This implies that I have to spend an extended amount of my time considering academics' work for publication in a particular issue of the journal. Besides the time-consuming aspect of article reviews, I also to deal with decisions that would, on the one hand, affront and/or disappoint many authors who submitted articles to the journal for consideration for publication, especially when articles receive undesirable reviews. On the other hand, I am also privileged to have read all the articles submitted to the journal for consideration for publication and gained valuable insight into the academic projects of especially university scholars.

I cannot recall that I have ever unjustifiably dismissed any journal article submitted for perusal and consideration for publication. Usually, my combined correspondence to potential authors has been to revise and perhaps resubmit their articles, and usually after another one or two rounds of reviews, the article was eventually accepted for publication in a next available issue. The journal publishes about six issues per year and each issue contains at least fifteen articles with the inclusion of a leading or introductory article. To my mind, I have been extremely accommodating as far as acceptance of journal articles is concerned. The overwhelming support I offer authors is one of avoidance and acceptance: avoidance in the sense that submissions should be academically rigorous, and arguments should lucid and coherent without a leaning towards exclusively descriptive pieces of writing. The *SAJHE* attempts to avoid publications that are merely descriptive and technically sound. Yet, I am always interested in articles that accentuated narratives with rich theoretical insights, lucidity and coherence. Acceptable articles, such as the latter, are always considered as apposite for appearance in the *SAJHE* because I always hold the view that articles that are theoretically insightful can make meaningful contributions to discourses in and about higher education. In other words, I remain attuned to the exercise of rhythmic caring in the eventual acceptance of pieces of writing, simultaneously trying to avoid pedantic and less rigorous pieces of work.

I do not deny that my focus was on academic rigour and an advancement of scholarship in and about higher education. However, I was not prejudiced towards those who wrote the article, but rather concentrated on what was articulated in manuscripts with the implications for higher education being highly prized. In other words, as one of the very few black journal editors in the country, I did not consider privileging black scholars as a reason for publication. Yet, I recognised, that in some instances, the work of some black academics had to be cared for more than others. And, it is in this regard, that my union with black scholarship enhanced to the extent that I became more conscious of publishing work in the fields of decoloniality and transformation in and about HE matters on the African continent. As a corollary of such an understanding and bias towards transformative work, I even published some special editions of the journal on decoloniality, transformation, criticality, and care within pedagogical encounters at African universities.

Of course, I do not deny that for many authors, publishing their work is a high priority because their research income and status, promotional opportunities and academic advancement often depend on whether their work has been considered good enough for publication. This rush towards publication instigated by a market-driven concern largely contributed to the commodification of knowledge interests. In a way, having one's work published in the *SAJHE* is therefore considered meritorious in some ways, yet, questions also arose about the lack of credibility of authors not having their work published in internationally recognised journals. However, I might add, for many African authors, the *SAJHE* is considered an international space for publication. Recently, increasing numbers of African scholars have found their way into publishing in the *SAJHE*. I am not intimating that publishing in international journals is more credible than publishing in local ones. Not at all. By going the international route, one invariably opens up your scholarly work to a wider audience, and perhaps going local seems to go against exposing one's work internationally, particularly on the African continent.

Nevertheless, what I have shown thus far, is that scholars' work can and should be treated with care. When article submissions seem to be a representation of incoherent and unsubstantiated assertions, journal editors should caringly point this out to especially emerging authors. In turn, such authors should earnestly consider the advice of editors so that resubmissions can once again be considered with the same rigour as previously. Of course, not everything can and should be published, but then again, if authors have made concerted efforts to revise and resubmit their work for consideration, editors are obliged to look at their work with greater care. I consider myself an editor who considers scholars' work with care, and I have been shown to be far more interested in enhancing the credibility of scholarly work rather than just succumbing to the intellectual game of publish or perish. By this, I mean that, as an editor, I would consider informing authors why their work merits publication, while those authors whose articles do not deserve to be placed in the *SAJHE* will be informed with kindness. I do not hold the view that harsh and dismissive comments should ever be sent to authors. However, I equally do not agree with a practice of informing authors whether their work lacks substance. Thus, my caring is enacted in relation to my comments that fluctuate between rigorous feedback pointing out the deficiencies in scholars' writing, and acknowledging when seminal work of others require commendation. In this way, the care that I brought to editorship can be framed as rhythmic. This brings me to a discussion of doctoral supervision over more than two decades in higher education.

Care and Supervision

Without hailing the number of PhDs I have supervised and examined over more than two decades, suffice to say that there were many who required substantial care, some more so than others. In a previous work (Waghid, 2015: 19–20), I spoke at length about my encounters with doctoral candidates and described it as a rhythmic dance:

Given the myriad shifts of thinking, strategies and back-and-forth debating with these students, I have referred to my encounters as a dance. While some encounters have been lucid, well-timed, and crisp, others have been rambling, at times even dizzying – not unlike a dance of varying pace and cadence. The doctoral encounter in motion: At times the student would wait for my next move, hoping I would lead, wanting me to lead, and as the dance routine improved the student would slowly take the lead, until the time where I was no longer needed to lead the dance. And while some dances have been focused as the twirling image of a dervish, others have been unsure as a first dance marred by stepping on the other's toes.

In capturing the moment in each of my rhythmic dances with students, I specifically accentuate my democratic educational encounters. On initiating my students into doctoral studies, I first introduce them to specific democratic educational theories I think would be relevant and supportive of their studies. I am particularly interested in the interpretations and analyses of such theories and how they (students) find relevance in theorists' seminal work in terms of their dissertations. As soon as students make sense of theories important to their work, they constantly engage with me about their understandings, and then construct and deconstruct their own narratives as they begin to situate their understandings of important seminal works in their writings. I recognise them as autonomous beings, capable of articulating their own arguments. Yet, at the same time, they have encountered a demanding promoter who insists that they produce justifiable claims in and through their work. In a different way, I recognise their humanity and by implication their fallibility as students and, and turn, they recognise the humanity in me. As aptly stated by Cavell (1979: 433), in human encounters, for instance, of a democratic kind, one's relationship with others is constituted by humanity, 'I have to acknowledge humanity in the other, and the basis of it seems to lie in me.'

I consider my supervision of students, mostly from the African continent, as a responsibility owed to humanity as the continent strives to produce morally just persons to cultivate Africa's young democracies. It so happens that almost all my doctoral students embark on their academic journeys in the field of democratic citizenship education, in particular, how such an understanding of education can be of relevance to their specific educational contexts. What I want them to do is to make sense of notions such as democratic iterations, citizenship rights and cosmopolitan justice in the production of their theses. In all my supervision, I connect students to issues of civility, plurality, disagreement, equality, justice and difference – those issues that open them up to different others, in particular conceiving the other and otherness from their points of view and engaging them anew (Cavell, 1979: 441). In this way, I enact my responsibility to these students by disclosing intimacy with them. As Cavell (1979: 463) states, 'human beings do not necessarily desire isolation and incomprehension, but union or reunion, call it community'. By implication, it is not difficult for my students to pursue the argumentative route in their theses, that is, a way that contributes to their theses becoming theoretically rigorous. As I have noted elsewhere:

> [D]octoral studies should not ignore the technical and professional use of procedures of educational research, but I would advocate that less emphasis be placed on these techniques and more on arguments which should emanate as a result of using techniques. Often too many students write a chapter on techniques which seem to be unrelated to the arguments that ensue in dissertations. (Waghid, 2015: 130)

My encounters with students have always been open to taking risks, and still are. Students take risks on account of not being inhibited by me to articulate their thoughts. Equally, I take risks too by challenging students throughout their studies without having to anticipate their resentment towards me. In this way, our encounters are constituted by an ethic of care that allows both of us to remain responsive to one another.

In essence, through editorship and supervision, I have shown how rhythmic caring manifests in such encounters with authors and students respectively. Such encounters are never without dissonant action in the sense that discomfort, practical criticism and scepticism constitute such encounters. In the first instance, authors and students experience a sense of discomfort when they are informed that their writing requires substantial revisions. Equally, I experience some moments of discomfort in pointing out lapses within their arguments. Secondly, our collective encounters are instigated by moments of practical criticism. Authors and students experience rigorous feedback on their work. In response to my comments, they respond equally with more justifiable pieces of writing. Thirdly, in reviewing their work, I adopt an attitude of suspicion as I challenge them to make their claims more lucid and coherent. Likewise, I respond to their critical comments of me in the sense that they could clarify and provide more plausible arguments in their writing. The point I am making is that dissonant action invariably constitutes our encounters. Yet, through to-and-fro moments of rupturing and care – rhythmic care – the opportunity exists for authors and students to produce and reproduce more tenable pieces of writing. In other words, authors, students and I are provoked to become more critical and reflective in our encounters to produce more substantive pieces of scholarly work. In this way, our encounters are deepened by openness, reflexivity and provocation. That is to say, our encounters are underscored by rhythmic caring through dissonance – a view of caring I have developed in more detail elsewhere (Davids & Waghid, 2018). In the next section, I focus on my term as dean in a faculty of education in relation to a notion of rhythmic care.

Deanship and Care

As with many academics working in an HE environment, upward mobility in relation to the academic profession is often associated with people's leadership and management capacities. I have always thought of myself as meticulous and hardworking. This means that a deanship did not necessarily undermine my academic pursuits at a university. Having been inspired by a previous dean in the faculty who considered 'doing things for others' as important to his deanship, I aspired towards a deanship in the faculty where I still work on the grounds that I thought that, in addition to its meritorious acclaim, a deanship would allow me to work with others in doing things for a faculty that requires transformation in terms of both its academic project as well as its human resources. Simply put, a faculty cannot just be concerned about producing publication outputs and student throughputs without also being equally interested in the cultivation of acts of transformation. Likewise, transformation can also not be about changing the demographic profile of a faculty, more importantly, it also has to enhance scholarship in diversity. As it turned out to be, our faculty has been credited for many years after my deanship as a highly transformed faculty in terms of its demographic profile. However, although my interests were mainly the diversification of scholarship and ways of understanding events in the world, much of my deanship became associated with a push for numbers. Notwithstanding, research outputs escalated during my term as dean and many faculty staff were intent on producing outputs within the context of their disciplines. If there was one failure during my deanship, I think, it was that the quest for individual success became increasingly prioritised as academics saw one another as competitors rather than collaborators in the production of scholarly work. My deanship cannot be faulted for this scenario alone as the HE context simply demands that academics produce.

Under my leadership, there seemed to have been an intellectual credibility, which became associated with our faculty, and executive management looked favourably upon our research endeavours. No longer were we considered merely as some kind of teacher training institute. Instead, the demands for quality teaching and learning became more and more pronounced and, often, the strength of the research by our faculty was used by our critics to assess some of the academic loopholes regarding teaching and learning. However, many staff members showed that with success at the level of educational research came an overwhelming improvement in teaching and learning. This makes sense, because quality teaching and learning are constituted by research 'excellence'. This situation in turn resulted in the faculty being referred to as highly successful in terms of its research, despite an increase in the diversity of staff. The cliché that diversity enhances excellence became associated with the work done in the faculty under my leadership. My understanding was that, unless academics cared for their scholarship, they would not contribute favourably and justifiably to an increase in research productivity – a view shared by a few at the time. Yet, this view of enhanced scholarship through diversity was not shared by the entire staff. There were many staff members who felt that the drive by the faculty towards enhanced research productivity would work against its research excellence. I do not hold this view as with an increase in the number of publications, the possibility is always there for quality to be enhanced because the numbers are there. How can one have quality outputs in the first place, if there are no tangible numbers in the publication units? I completed a term of deanship with great optimism that our faculty would sustain its research productivity. Of course, it did, in many ways. However, our teaching and learning seemed to have suffered considerably on account of producing quality programmes and enhanced teaching and learning. I do not think research productivity can and should ever be blamed for a lack of credible teaching and learning, for that in itself would mark the end of educational research. However, with hindsight, more patience perhaps should be exercised towards those who require much more assistance than others, as university faculties endeavour to increase their productivity. In short, care ought to be exercised rhythmically so that research productivity cannot and should not be used as an excuse for a lack of credible teaching and learning.

On the Ethical Responsibility of Rhythmic Caring: Decoloniality, Transformation and a Pedagogy of Bearing Witness

Inasmuch as rhythmic caring has been shown to be an enabling practice within higher education, it can by no means be considered a sufficient practice within any pedagogical action. It is my contention that higher education on the African continent is at a stage where the rationale for doing educational research – such as publishing and doctoral education – can no longer just be pursued for its own sake. Such a view of HE research would not only be inattentive to societal developments on the continent, but it will also be remiss of performing a significant transformative role, considering our colonial and apartheid past. Implicit in a practice of rhythmic caring is an understanding that higher education is a public good, and any defective understanding of the practice of higher education ought to be remedied. By implication, academics within an HE context cannot remain oblivious of their ethical responsibility to enact the necessary change.

In the next section, I offer some explication on why ethical responsibility on the part of academics on the African continent cannot be blind to embarking on decoloniality, transformation and a pedagogy of witnessing.

Firstly, in line with Chinua Achebe's (1989: 86) explication of decoloniality, where he considers the practice of decoloniality as a human pursuit of epistemic justice, I cannot imagine any act of caring to be remiss of the ethical responsibility to move beyond that which suffers from freedom, equality and justice. In my view, academic writing and doctoral scholarship cannot be blind to a pursuit of freedom, equality and justice. What follows from such an understanding of decoloniality, is that academic pursuits – certainly on the African continent – are dependent on people who are ethically obliged to act responsibly in defence of what N'gugi Wa'Thiongo (2012: 6) refers to as, the marginalised, and the future of the global world. Being concerned with the marginalised – my deanship at the time was concerned with the inclusion of the marginalised in the HE realm – and by implication, the future of the global world implies that academic pursuits cannot be only the domain of the privileged few. I often hear within circles of the academe in South Africa, that established universities are concerned with the large number of white academics, mostly men, who will leave the profession in under a decade which, it is communicated, will leave a huge vacuum in academic research. Of course, any HE system that loses its researchers should be concerned, especially if those very researchers have been responsible for having overwhelmingly contributed to its research productivity. However, inasmuch as such a situation seems alarming, what would even be more dissatisfying would be for HEIs to do very little to advance the levels of scholarship of its previously marginalised groups, in particular women and blacks academics. By implication, intellectual pursuits that gain a strong decolonial impetus are more inclined to advance the scholarly interests of the broader African continent than being strictly concerned to retain those academics who have been privileged in the past and who have built their success on such opportune academic freedoms. Of course, unless, privileged academics strongly put the scholarly interests of the marginalised first, such endeavours should not be prioritised by practices of decoloniality.

Secondly, the idea of transformation in African higher education is not new. Of course, racial and class imbalances in relation to academic appointments have been very prevalent on the African continent since the days of colonialism. However, what has emerged as a notable discussion point in terms of university academic appointments has been the issue surrounding the appointment of previously disadvantaged black staff. Undeniably, demographic change at HE level does not necessarily imply that institutions would have immediately shifted previously held views on, say pedagogical matters. Yet, in many instances, merely having changed the demographic profile of institutions resulted in a resistance to change. Here, I specifically think of several previously disadvantaged staff who merely perpetuated the status quo of unjust teaching and learning, even at times aggravating unfreedom and inequality in higher education at several universities on the African continent, on the one hand. On the other hand, however, having appointed more diverse black staff in the HE sector also advantaged higher education in the sense that, for instance, educational research for that matter, became more credible and substantive than the previously published work. Here, I think of my own faculty, which enhanced its reputation as a research-oriented academic institution with the appointment of more staff from previously disadvantaged communities over the past decade. Even at the level of advancing, issues of recognition and diversity in pedagogical matters have gained considerable momentum in the faculty where I work over the past twenty years. In this sense, demographic diversity has significantly enhanced what has customarily become known as quality educational research to the extent that the institution itself would refer to the co-existing of quality and diversity in the faculty of education. The point is, with more freedom, openness and an exercise of equality, educational research became more substantive and diverse, which is a testimony to the success of transformation within higher education.

Thirdly, showing love and care within higher education, is a significant exercise of virtue in the sense that academics experience care when they themselves commit to enacting care. Higher education in Africa needs to care because for too long, academics at institutions of higher learning have absolved themselves in many ways from the challenges that confront African societies. I do not think that university academics should be freed from their ethical responsibility to care for their communities. This implies doing educational research that is responsive to the predicaments that beset their communities on the continent. Academics should no longer just occupy neutral educational spaces that suggest their work should remain unrelated to the dilemmas within African societies. That is, academics have an ethical responsibility and should earnestly endeavour to address the societal dilemmas that plague human living – a matter of bearing witness through pedagogy. The point I am making is that academics cannot be oblivious of enacting their ethical responsibilities within the societies where they live. If academics ignore some of the dystopias in African societies, they would not be fulfilling their roles as responsible ethical beings. If academics are not prepared to speak out against escalating levels of crime, human trafficking, environmental degradation, climate change, deforestation, drug abuse and violence, then who should? I cannot imagine that we should leave the dystopias to be attended to by political, religious and other community leaders, as if such dystopias have nothing to do with higher education. If our scholarly writings cannot be in condemnation of bigotry, hatred and oppression, then what is our writing worth?

Once again, I am reminded of the almost countless number of PhDs and master's theses that seldom address relevant dystopias in our communities. Ethical responsibility demands that students and academics collectively work in an attempt to undermine the dystopias that have manifested in African communities. And, it is in the latter regard that our scholarly work becomes much more than just writing for recognition and profitable gain. We ought to care more for ourselves and the communities that shape us. Paulo Freire (2001: 128–129) aptly reminds us that caring educative practices are not only intellectually thoughtful and autonomous human practices, but also ethical and political actions constituted by concerns of humanity and justice. Such human encounters, following Freire (2001: 126), are 'capable of awakening, stimulating, and developing in us a taste for caring and for joy, without which educative practice has no meaning at all'. If the above happens, university academics would bear witness within and through their pedagogical encounters. Cultivating a pedagogy of bearing witness has some connection with being a witness for change. And, when changed is witnessed, it is enacted and one's ethical responsibility is entirely oriented towards the cultivation of just and humane acts – that is, those virtuous moments that will contribute towards reimagining the HE system on the African continent. In other words, bearing witness is an act of committing oneself to bring about change rather than waiting on others to actuate change. Bearing witness implies that university scholarship should be driven by change agents with an intent to produce transformation within their communities.

Pursuant to the afore-mentioned argument, African university academics cannot pursue educational research agendas without being oblivious of past and present abominations such as mutilation, the use of child soldiers, detention camps, mass rapes, endless conflict, civil wars, crimes against humanity, cannibalism, genocide, hunger, HIV and AIDS, the lack of medical care, and the disarray of many immigrants. Drawing on the work of French award-winning author, Pascal Brucker (2010), I want to offer three distinct ways in which caring can be used in higher education to respond to some of the abominations mentioned above that are still prevalent on the African continent. Firstly, reconciliatory talk – as an act of caring for humanity – ought to become a central feature within deliberations in and about higher education. Such a process should promise perpetrators of heinous crimes – if the law allows it – immunity in return for revealing truth. Such a view of reconciliation is premised on the idea that even the worst perpetrators of crimes against humanity can have their dignity restored as human beings instead of being subjected to acts of vengeance and public humiliation (Brucker, 2010: 212). The aim of reconciliatory talk as cogently put by Brucker (2010: 212), 'is to use mutual gestures to bring victims and tormentors divided by and inexpiable hatred closer together'. The Truth and Reconciliation Commission (TRC) in South Africa is a poignant example of putting an end to intractable quarrels, and 'providing that the bitterest heritages can be overcome' (Brucker, 2010: 214).

Secondly, Brucker's (2010: 141) idea of listening to the suffering of others – a matter of acting caringly – is an appropriate way by which HE practitioners can begin to make sense of and even constructively address major societal concerns, especially those peoples victimised and humiliated by dominant others. Here, I am specifically referring to listening to those peoples who have been stained ignominiously by acts of deportation, torture, enslavement, horror, violent terror, brutality and criminality. Through listening to the suffering of others, HE practitioners would begin to restitute the phenomenon of human adversity. As Brucker (2010: 166) states:

[To eradicate] potential barbarity – racism, anti-Semitism, machismo, homophobia [and] to extricate ourselves from this situation will be of no use without a mixture of determination and generosity [i.e. caring]. We have to repress the most hardened ruffians and treat the others in a brotherly way, getting them out of this cycle of failure and violence. If we don't, most of them will remain a lost generation, inevitably oscillating between prison, the mafias, and the Islamists.

Thirdly, as an act of care, HE practitioners ought to deepen and intensify the practice of democratic engagement (Brucker, 2010: 219). To address some of the dystopias of today, teaching and learning have to become more attentive 'to listen[ing] and debate, [without] the risk of feeding the flames we are trying to put out' (Brucker, 2010: 2018). When people rediscover its civilizing capacity of democratic engagement they would at once speak out against its taste for blood, carnage and shame. By injecting the spirit of democratic and critical engagement into its human encounters, people would not only contribute to saving humanity from the perils of inhumanity and injustice, but would contribute also to 'the survival of humanity' (Brucker, 2010: 221). If the aforementioned happens, caring would have manifested within HE discourses.

Summary

In this chapter, I have offered a reflective account of my caring relations with authors, students and faculty staff. In such instances, my encounters have been informed by an ethic of care that resonates with being attentive, responsive and attuned to those with whom I engaged. Inasmuch as I assumed the role of carer in the encounters, I did not remain oblivious that the recipients of care also confirmed my encounter with them as one of openness, trust and critical engagement – those virtues of caring that always allow rhythm to unfold in dissonant pedagogical encounters.

In a way, this chapter illustrated that academic inquiry itself can be enhanced through an ethic of care (Nelsen, 2013: 351). The point is, the caring relationship among students, authors, fellow academics and myself is intertwined with academic pursuits 'embodied as involving the body-mind'

(Nelsen, 2013: 367). In other words, through the writing of publications and doctoral supervision of students, rationality and affect are practiced inseparably within the academic inquiry and, as aptly put by Nelsen (2013: 367), 'are always present in our caring encounters'. In his words:

> Educationally, the implication is that the inquiry of care also entails the shared project of exploring what it means to care about an idea, an area of study, a question, a passion. Specifically, the inquiry of care involves developing relations with the objects of inquiry – whether they are physical objects or ideas. The inquiry of care also stresses that such engagement is fully embodied, that is, that students ... are fully embodied beings who engage in inquiry with their intellects, their emotions, and their bodies. (Nelsen, 2013: 367)

Finally, inasmuch as our relations of care have been rhythmic, our academic pursuits are embodied because, firstly, our academic inquiry attended to the relationships between authors, students, academics and myself; and secondly, the academic pursuits within themselves have been aesthetically linked to our reasons and affections.

References

Achebe, C. (1989). *Hopes and impediments: Selected essays*. New York: Anchor Books.

Brucker, P. (2010). *The tyranny of guilt: An essay on Western masochism*. Princeton, NJ: Princeton University Press.

Cavell, S. (1979). *The claim of reason: Wittgenstein, skepticism, morality, and tragedy*. Oxford, UK: Oxford University Press.

Davids, N., & Waghid, Y. (2018). *Teaching and learning as a pedagogic pilgrimage: Cultivating faith, hope and imagination*. London. New York: Routledge.

Freire, P. (2001). *Pedagogy of freedom: Ethics, democracy, and civic courage*. Lanham, MD: Rowman & Littlefield.

Nelsen, P. (2013). The inquiry of care. *Educational Theory, 63*(4), 351–367.

Waghid, Y. (2015). *Dancing with doctoral encounters: Democratic education in motion*. Stellenbosch, South Africa: Sun Press.

Wa'Thiongo, N. (2012). *Globalectics: Theory and the politics of knowing*. New York: Columbia University Press.

12

Cultivating Care: Towards a Philosophy of Higher Education in Africa

Introduction

Considering a chapter on a philosophy of higher education in Africa should be understood in the context of a concern expressed by Aaron Stoller and Eli Kramer (2018: 1) 'that no moderate debate or meaningful scholarship developed around the idea of curriculum in higher education … [can do without] talk of curriculum [that] is framed exclusively within the context of teaching methods for content delivery'. What I have attempted to do in this book, is to develop a concept of care in the context of rhythm that could influence pedagogical encounters positively. And, in a way, a particular philosophy of higher education has been implicitly argued for without engaging the criticism that pedagogical encounters within higher education in Africa 'do not offer robust, critical imaginaries capable of constructing institutions of higher learning' (Stoller & Kramer, 2018: 3). Unlike some philosophers who are accused of producing works in higher education detached from 'the material and political conditions of institutions' (Stoller & Kramer, 2018: 4), I have framed this book in the interest of a sensitivity towards the epistemic, organisational, social and political cultures of higher education. In this way, hopefully, I can prepare students to become inclusive, attentive, democratic, empathic and just within and through pedagogical encounters in higher education. Like Stoller and Kramer (2018: 15), I attempt to reconstruct a philosophy of higher education. However, my attempt in reconstructing such a philosophy is linked to thinking caringly and rhythmically in and about pedagogical encounters. As corroborated by Stoller and Kramer (2018: 15), a reconstructive philosophy of higher education 'must consider … the project of teaching and learning … as well as the relationship between pedagogy and disciplinary research'. This chapter is an attempt to move towards a reconstructive notion of higher education in Africa in relation to teaching and learning within higher education.

Teaching and Learning as Embodied Pedagogy

Like Thaddeus Metz (2018: 161) who avers that higher education in Africa is dependent on the sub-Saharan philosophical tradition of relationality and communality, I want to make a case for higher education constituted by a plausible understanding of ethical caring. Metz (2018: 163) argues that a sub-Saharan notion of morality underscored by communal relationships with human persons and relationality merits pursuit for their own sake. For him, sub-Saharan Africa considers the idea of 'life-force, roughly, and invisible energy that has come from God, as basic to African ethical thought', which ought to be the guiding principle for any understanding of higher education (Metz, 2018: 163). Not misrecognising the latter view, I am somewhat more attracted to his view that solidarity with others or caring for their quality of life – *ubuntu* – and being empathically aware of others, in particular respecting the dignity of others through communion, ought to constitute the notion of an embodied pedagogy (Metz, 2018: 167). Put differently, an embodied pedagogy is constituted by an ethic of care that requires of humans to work in solidarity, and to respect one another's dignity. When an embodied pedagogy is pursued within African higher education, pedagogical encounters – most notably teaching and learning – will be drawn to communality where teachers and students will enable one another to act with love and friendliness that will cause them to cooperate willingly and to cohere irrespective of their differences (Metz, 2018: 166). The aim of such embodied encounters is especially geared 'to help students from lower economic classes acquire the qualifications needed to compete for jobs and other positions and to obtain the rewards that are attached to them' (Metz, 2018: 167). In other words, providing equal opportunity instead of pure meritocracy is considered an act of care in terms of which public universities ought to accommodate those economically disadvantaged students within the African HE sector. It is a matter of embodying care for oneself and others: caring for oneself is about advancing a cause that depends on one's attunement to the disadvantaged, while caring for others would help others improve their situations in day-to-day life.

In the above regard, I am reminded of an initiative undertaken by Stellenbosch University's Centre for Pedagogy (SUNCEP). Students who have performed inadequately in their final year of schooling, can apply to the university for acceptance into the SUNCEP SciMatUS (Science and Mathematics at Stellenbosch University) programme. Many of the students are registered for a pre-university year to improve their results in science and mathematics, together with communication and life skills. On completion of the programme they are then placed at various faculties of their choice, such as engineering, medicine, law and education. It was found that students who successfully completed a year at SciMatUS are better prepared to cope with the demands of university life. This example shows that if some students, mostly from disadvantaged communities, are supported and afforded equal opportunities to study at a university, they would be more favourably positioned to succeed. By far the majority of SciMatUS students eventually go on to complete a formal university qualification. Through an embodied pedagogy, students are cared for and life-changing opportunities are afforded them to be educationally successful. By implication, a university curriculum cannot be exclusively related to content and pedagogy in a parochial way. The example of SUNCEP shows that a university curriculum can be embodied where teachers and students work in communion to embark on teaching and learning that enhance the dignity of those who need it more than others – a matter of having embodied a pedagogy that addresses the educational needs of students. The point about an embodied curriculum or pedagogy is that it is constituted by a 'life force' – a rationale – of caring for others in the same way one perhaps cares for yourself. It is not that one merely recognises that others are in need of care. Rather, in recognition of a need to care, people actually embark on caring for others whom they consider as mostly in need of care. The rationale for caring is guided by a desire to actuate change in the lives of others and oneself. For once, one does not just act alone in taking care of others. Instead one is driven by an understanding of communion with others towards whom you have a responsibility to ensure that their life worlds are improved. Such a form of caring is not a matter of doing something *for* others that could improve their situation. Rather one does things *with* others for the sake of enhancing others' often undesirable circumstances. Care is embodied. Thus, caring *with* others grows out of an understanding that people ought to act communally. In doing so, they would be most appropriately attuned to connect with and care with one another as they communally endeavour to change their undesirable situations.

Towards Deliberative Engagement, Criticality and Cultural Agency

Elsewhere (see Waghid, Waghid, & Waghid, 2018: 31) it is argued that teaching and learning at African universities ought to become more deliberative and critical if Africans are to move beyond economic underdevelopment, social inequality and political instability. The latter view is partially supported by Stoller and Kramer (2018: 18) who posit, '[w]ithout a critical and theoretical language, we can neither conceptualize (and therefore meaningfully reconstruct) our practice, nor can we resist outside forces, particularly in the context of teaching, learning, and knowing'. In other words, without a credible philosophy of teaching and learning in African higher education, HE practitioners would be 'simply unable to imagine alternatives to practice because we see our pedagogical and institutional labor as a theoretical dead zone' (Stoller & Kramer, 2018: 18). Why? In the first place, a philosophy of higher education brings teachers, managers and students into a discourse of deliberative inquiry where they attentively listen to what one another has to say about a range of matters such as the relevance or not of the curriculum, and whether university programmes are oriented toward an enactment of socially just concerns. Through such a form of inquiry, participants would not only be in a position to speak their minds about curricular matters but they would also make judgements about the feasibility of such issues for the political, economic and societal advancement of African communities. And, as deliberative engagement requires, such judgements can be in opposition to what have been articulated by others on the grounds that engagement is linked to an articulation of difference and dissent. Secondly, a philosophy of higher education that constitutes embodied teaching and learning calls for bringing into question and proffering alternative perspectives on curricular matters. By implication, considering that theoretical enhancement depends both on deliberation and on a critical take on curricular issues, any university programme development devoid of such necessary actions would invariably suffer from theoretical carelessness.

In addition to making university curricular concerns more attentive to care, deliberative engagement and criticality alone would not necessarily ensure caring pedagogical relations. In a previous work, *African philosophy of education reconsidered: On being human* (Waghid, 2014: 21–22), I argue in defence of a communitarian, reasonable and culture-dependent view of African philosophy of education. Such a philosophy of education does not only create opportunities for human engagement; it also engenders spaces for participants to be reasonably and culturally engaged. Reasonable engagement involves listening caringly and reflectively, whereas cultural engagement is concerned with a 'broader range of expressions, gestures, touches and other kinds of communication of Africa's peoples as they endeavor to interact in their social contexts, [and] mutually explore, and negotiate the pursuit of common understanding' (Waghid, 2014: 27). The point about bringing cultural agency into play within pedagogical encounters is that participants would at once be concerned with both someone's reasons as well as his or her cultural justifications for matters of interest to human encounters. The latter of course, requires that one does not have to listen only to what others have to say, but also to what they espouse, and to the justifications they proffer in defence of their cultural claims. For instance, learning that only focuses on a theoretical discourse that describes its value without taking into account students' cultural agency would remain devoid of any form of authentic learning (Stroller & Kramer, 2018: 18). African communities make much of culture on the grounds that human enactments do not occur independently from their traditions and cultural ways of seeing the world. They endeavour to bring their local understandings of events into conversation with world-wide events and then make judgements about improving life for its citizens (Waghid, 2014). Africans' rationality is not just about the level of articulations and justifications. Instead, its rational justifications of this or that matter are inextricably connected to their very being and the cultural identities of people. It is not a matter of culture taking precedence over rational argumentation. Rather, for Africans, rational argumentation would be much more enriched if their cultural labour were taken stock of, even when they proffer rational justifications for their points of view. This brings me to a discussion of responsibility and justice in relation to a philosophy of higher education for Africa.

On Responsibility, Epistemic Justice and Change

Any philosophy of higher education has to be able to respond to something or a situation if it warrants being referred to as a philosophy of education. This is so on the grounds that a philosophy of education is a human activity that involves what people do and become. When people are able to do this or that it means that they can enable something to unfold. And, when they respond to something or a situation, it implies that they have put their ability into action for the sake of responding to a matter. In the same way, any form of education requires of humans to engage and become this or that. The point I am making, is that any philosophy of higher education for Africa involves humans exerting their capacities in such a way that they become responsive to matters or situations on the African continent. Consequently, a philosophy of higher education for Africa ought to be associated primarily with the responsibility of such a discourse to the continent of Africa. For instance, a philosophy of higher education in Africa ought to be concerned about and responsive to Africa's predicaments. If one considers that some of Africa's dystopias involve ethnic conflict, malnutrition, hunger and drought, the spreading of HIV and AIDS, children being used as war soldiers, and human trafficking, then the responsibility of a philosophy of higher education in Africa is to enact ways by which the dystopias can be combatted. What follows from the afore-mentioned discussion, is that a philosophy of higher education in Africa has a responsibility to address the above dilemmas associated with human life on the continent.

Likewise, as a philosophy of higher education in Africa endeavours to respond to Africa's problems; such a philosophy of education therefore ought to do so to rectify injustice. According to Metz (2018: 172):

> Another facet of effecting redress is likely to involve seeking to make up for epistemic injustice, that is, finding ways to do right by people insofar as they had been treated discordantly in respect of their ways of interpreting the world. In the first instance, and most easily, this would mean changing the curriculum to include neglected or denigrated works … In the ideal case, a university would reflect on respects in which current practices (perhaps unintentionally) occlude engagement with suppressed cultures.

My interest is in a philosophy of higher education in Africa that responds justly to multiple cultures through university curricula. In my own field of inquiry, for too long, philosophies of higher education in Africa have been too much concerned with works of established Anglo-Saxon and/or Francophone traditions. Not much attention has been given to philosophies of higher education in Africa that include the work of leading African scholars who have ably and responsibly addressed curriculum concerns on the continent. I am specifically thinking of works that accentuate the importance of decolonising a higher curriculum in Africa. For once, any HE curriculum that remains oblivious of decoloniality, for instance, seems to misrecognise the pedagogical harm that oppressive and hegemonic education have done on the continent. For this reason, a philosophy of higher education in Africa ought to become more concerned with a decoloniality project. If the latter happens, in the words of Metz (2018: 169), 'a university might teach students, say, how to become more aware of their implicit biases, how to identify and deal with conflicts of interest, and how to become more attuned to others' points of view and feelings'. In short, such a university would care for its students because its philosophy of higher education has a direct bearing on cultivating what is good for Africa and the world.

Without trivialising the notion of decoloniality, as it is profoundly associated with breaking away from Africa's colonial and post-colonial past, I want to give more credence to this idea of decoloniality in the context of the concept of *shahadah* or bearing witness to which I alluded briefly in the previous chapter. As enunciated in the Islamic tradition, *shahadah* or bearing witness is a necessary and enabling condition for human action. Every Muslim individual irrespective of cultural persuasion or sectarian preference – such as Sunni'sm or Shi'sm (two dominant Muslim sectarian groups in the world today) – ought to commit him- or herself to his or her faith through the enunciation of *shahadah* or *kalimah* – that is, to bear witness. In full, *kalimah* reads as follows:

> *Ash hadu alla ilaha illalahi wa ashadu anna muhammadan rasulu allah* (I bear witness that there is no deity but Allah and I bear witness that the Prophet Muhammad (peace and blessings be upon him) is the messenger of Allah).

One would not find a single Muslim person in this world who denies the *kalimah*. It is regarded as the most fundamental dimension of the belief of a Muslim. At least three dimensions of faith are constitutive of *shahadah*. Firstly, a person's conviction of belief is directed only to a singular Being, considered by Muslims as the Most Beneficent (*al-Rahman*) and the Most Compassionate (*al-Rahim*). To pay reverence to a Being that is considered both the holder and provider of compassion is tantamount to acknowledging that having faith is an act of compassion according to which a human devotes his or her entire life towards the recognition and cultivation of compassion. The point is that it is not possible to revere someone for being the ultimate provider of compassion yet as a human – a creation of this Ultimate Being – one does not enact compassion oneself. Thus, for a Muslim to venerate Allah, one is always drawn to acting compassionately. Secondly, when a Muslim bears witness that the Prophet of Islam is a Messenger of Allah, he or she at once recognises that the life experiences (*Sunnah*) of the Prophet embody compassion. Simply put, compassion is not just an act that belongs to a transcendental realm; rather, it is an act that can be performed by humans as the Prophet of Islam was human. By implication, according to the concept of *shahadah*, compassion is always embodied within and through the actions of humans. One does not have to wait for some transcendental act to unfold that could result in mercy being afforded humankind as a consequence of some spiritually endowed act. Instead, as an acknowledgement of *shahadah,* compassion is a human capacity that can be nurtured and enacted towards humanity, irrespective of people's faith or religious orientation. That is, the human body's embodiment of compassion is a vindication that such a virtue ought to be enacted in service always of humanity. Thirdly, *shahadah* is implicitly connected to an individual's commitment to withstand anything that works against compassion. This means that any form of human and non-human injustice cannot and should not be addressed without compassion. Compassion is therefore an act of unconditional virtue. For Muslims, Allah does not require anything from humans in order to show compassion. Irrespective of how unsatisfactory the human condition might be compassion does not have any condition that needs to be satisfied before it is practised. When the Prophet Muhammad's beloved uncle died without having embraced Islam, compassion was not shown to him and family during bereavement on condition that he first had to become Muslim. Compassion is an unconditional act of humanity. In short, recognising compassion as an act of humanity, embodying it, and practicing it unconditionally seems to be an understanding of virtue that underscores a Muslim's utterance of *kalimah*. It is this framework of *shahadah* that I now use to show why and how decoloniality can and should be enacted within and through a philosophy of higher education.

Decoloniality as an Act of Compassion: Making Care Work

Throughout the book, I have accentuated the notion of compassion in relation to enacting care. I now offer a more detailed account of why and how compassion can be used to harness decoloniality in our attempts to enact a defensible philosophy of higher education in Africa. Firstly, compassion ought to be conceived as an act of humanity. This implies that compassion cannot just be used in preference of some individual or group of persons. Every individual by virtue of being human is eligible to be treated with compassion. Compassion, in this way, cannot simply be the ownership of someone or a few. Rather, compassion is due every single individual irrespective of his or her convictions, persuasions and ways of being. When I think about a philosophy of higher education in Africa that is constituted by the notion of compassion, then such a philosophy does not discriminate neither does it hold some people in higher esteem than others on account of their self-assumed cultural and ethnic privileges. People are people on the basis of being human and they cannot be withheld from experiencing compassion. Compassion is not given someone; instead, it is inherent to what it means to be human. Of course, the question can rightly be asked whether a person who acts monstrously towards others is still entitled to be treated with compassion. One could prevent the monstrous acts of a person. However, even in doing so, one should never withhold compassion from such a person as if one owns compassion. By virtue of being human one is obliged to be treated with compassion. Should those who blow up other humans be treated with compassion? Of course, there is always the possibility that humans could act humanely on the grounds that they are human and, hence, they cannot be denied compassion even if they act inhumanely themselves. If we care for humanity then our actions cannot be only retaliation and retribution indiscriminately without showing compassion. Even the person who has committed heinous crimes cannot be denied compassion as his or her humanity is inextricably connected to the virtue of compassion. Certainly, having been created by Allah means that the compassion Allah stands for cannot become the ownership of any other person. One's humanity and personhood are constitutive of compassion. What follows from the afore-mentioned, is that any philosophy of higher education in Africa ought to consider compassion as its rationale, for without it, there is no point in cultivating a higher education for Africa's peoples. Decoloniality, by implication, should be considered an act of compassion whereby university curricula and programmes ought to be designed and constructed in such a way that the core curricular offerings centralise compassionate human action. How else will Africans heal the scars of colonialism, oppression, racism and exclusion, if Africans are not going to be initiated into HE discourses that place compassion at its core?

Perhaps, to heal the scars of our tumultuous past – a past underscored by hatred and repression – compassion might just be the caring act of humanity that might advance Africa's development and concomitantly its caring HE discourses.

Secondly, embodying compassion implies that such a virtue is an act of quintessential human embodiment. This means that humans use their will in a self-directed way to do this or that. As aptly stated by Andros Loizou (2018), human embodiment is an act of wilfully directing the self towards the pursuit of truth, openness to others' experiences, and to deep human interrelationships. The exercise of human will in relation to compassion implies that humans ought to be willing to show compassion. And, by showing it, they are acting wilfully to make it happen. When compassion becomes a wilful act of human action, then humans would not be reluctant to enact it. They would embody compassion. Nowadays, several migrants from various northern African countries seek their way into European countries. Unless governments show willingness to act compassionately towards humans who experience upheavals and torment in their countries of origin, this human catastrophe will not be addressed adequately. Likewise, embodying compassion is to act openly towards others. When one shows openness, one embraces others into one's sphere of care without withholding your inner feelings of compassion towards them. In other words, through being open, one makes others realise that you understand their moment of grief and respond caringly towards them. One embodies compassion when you open yourself up to others in recognition of their arduous situation. In this way, one enhances your interrelationships with others who require your care. It is in this regard, by opening up to migrants that one's compassion for them deepens. But then, compassion has to become an act of human embodiment. In turn, decoloniality as an act of embodying compassion ought to encourage university administrators to open up equal access for previously disadvantaged students wilfully to pursue university studies. And, when such students are at the universities, they should be supported through mentorships throughout their years of study. Only then can university education for such students become a worthwhile decolonial experience – that is, an experience of compassionate embodiment.

Thirdly, at the time of writing this section on the unconditionality of compassion, I visited the Alhambra fortress-palace in Granada, Spain considered by many as Europe's jewel of Muslim architecture. Having lived in the city of Granada for a short while, I decided to walk from my apartment to the Alhambra, which I could see from the balcony of my apartment. When I started my walk up to the Alhambra, I could only marvel at the beautiful scenic route overwhelmed by the lush green leaves covering the entire pathway towards the entrance. After I had bought a ticket (and being lucky to get one as tickets are sold out in advance), I walked straight to the Generalife gardens and palaces once occupied by sultans and kings. Once inside, what fascinated me as I looked up to the walls and ceilings of the Alhambra, were the intricately carved Arabic inscriptions that adorn them. While gazing at the walls of the Alhambra, I could recognise many inscriptions of '*Wa la ghalib illallah*' – there is no victor but God. I came to learn that this particular inscription practically dominates 'the architectural canvas of the Alhambra visually, spatially and semantically' (Puerta Vilchez, 2010: 19). Of relevance to this book on caring, is a specific inscription, namely *Allahu khayrun hafithan wa huwa arhamu al-rahimin* – God is the best to take care, and He is the Most Compassionate of those who show compassion, which adorns some of the chambers of the palaces (Puerta Vilchez, 2010: 233). Despite Granada's fall to the Christians in 1492, the Alhambra's unique inscriptions and aesthetic beauty were retained, and what intrigued me most during my visit, was that such a magnificent piece of Muslim architecture was always kept in place by what it stands for – that is, a fortress-palace of unconditional commitment to a belief in an Omnipotent God (Allah) who inspired people of the past to search for happiness and to imbue themselves with compassion. As I looked up into the skies of Granada with the Alhambra at my feet, only one thought permeated my mind: if the Alhambra's architectural splendour could survive, then surely the Arabic inscriptions pertaining to care, happiness and compassion ought to occupy one's life unconditionally. What is it about such unconditional acts of compassion and happiness that are so inspirationally linked to care and caring about the world and its inhabitants in much the same way the Alhambra symbolises for me such acts of virtue?

Unconditional compassion implies that people are recognised on account of the vulnerabilities they experience without conditions attached to it. People are recognised for the vulnerabilities they encounter, and then they are assisted in such a way that their vulnerabilities are attended to caringly. Compassion is a virtue of unconditionality on the grounds that humans express their gratitude for their very existence by showing compassion towards others. In other words, the virtue of compassion does not require of humans to act in specific ways before they are shown compassion. Rather, whenever there is a vulnerability shown by humans they are treated compassionately without any conditions. When migrants are refused to enter the borders of another country, such a country does not extend unconditional compassion to them. That is, they are refused for this or that reason, and their circumstances remain dire, such as having to face torment and possible torture in their own countries of origin. When unconditional compassion is showed to migrants, they are allowed access to the countries where they choose to seek asylum without any conditions. They are allowed entry to countries of their choice on the grounds that others find their situation so severe that they are accepted as asylum seekers on the grounds of compassion. The reason why migrants should be granted asylum on compassionate grounds is based on the premise that happiness should not be denied them. They should be allowed happiness in the same way nationals enjoy citizenship, security and belonging in the countries in which they live.

Put differently, happiness for migrants implies that others should be attentive to their needs in the same way they recognise their own safety and security in the countries where they themselves are permanent residents. It is such acts of unconditional compassion and happiness that seem to be strongly linked to the practice of decoloniality. When unconditionality prevails, the possibility for decoloniality would invariably be enhanced on the grounds that moving beyond coloniality and post-coloniality requires of people to act without conditions. One cannot presume that decoloniality ought to become a restricted practice. Instead, it should be recognised that coloniality enslaved, dominated and excluded people from enacting their lives freely. Therefore, to un-enslave, un-dominate and un-exclude humans do not require of them to behave according to certain conditions. They ought to experience decoloniality without any conditions. And, if a philosophy of higher education in Africa were to be guided by unconditionality, then decoloniality on the continent might more appropriately find its way into pedagogical encounters where deliberations about possibility and opportunity for others might be vigorously defended. Like my visit to the Alhambra denotes, especially having observed the countless inscriptions in reference to faith and compassion, humans cannot be remiss of their ethical responsibility to care *with* others. If there is one aspect that stands out about my visit to the Alhambra, it is that humans have a brief lifespan and their dominance is temporary. What is left behind is what matters and, in this instance, it was the awareness that life will pass us all by and it is of no practical value to undermine and misrecognise one another. This immediately reminds me of the unnecessary wars and conflict that prevail in many parts of the world today. One nation wants to dominate others as if the only way that humans can live their lives is to be subjected to others' dominance and control. Therefore, it makes sense to offer compassion to every human being for what keeps us in solidarity, as humanity is our capacity to act humanely and therefore caringly. Any philosophy of higher education in Africa will be much appraised if constituted by such notions of care – a care that will remain unconditionally attuned to enacting compassion.

Summary

In this chapter, I have made an argument for a philosophy of higher education in Africa that ought to be constituted by embodied actions such as deliberative inquiry, criticality, cultural agency, responsibility, epistemic justice, and unconditional compassion. Without such an understanding of higher education in Africa, meaningful change would not ensue. This is so because the embodied actions mentioned above would enhance the capacities of students and teachers to think autonomously and enact epistemically just change. Only through such actions will 'the caring for people's quality of life' (Metz, 2018: 177) be taken seriously. A philosophy of higher education in Africa that draws on embodied actions will enhance the possibility of making Africa relevant to global thought in and about education. As aptly stated by Metz (2018: 182):

[T]he African philosophical tradition has highlighted the goods of relationship in ways that the Western one has not. Westerners, including Western *theorists*, routinely appreciate the values of identity and solidarity, but Western *theories* of higher education by and large neglect these values, often treating them merely as a means towards the practical end of self-governance (at either the individual or political level) and the intellectual end of understanding nature.

What follows from the above, is that embodied human actions constituted by virtues of deliberation, autonomy, justice and unconditional compassion, envelop what it means to implement a philosophy of higher education in Africa. Such a philosophy of higher education would be most favourably positioned to address aspirations of humans towards the cultivation of decoloniality – that is, a necessary and enabling practice in order for higher education and pedagogy in particular to become manifest on the African continent. Although the Alhambra and its surroundings in the Spanish city of Granada signify the transfer of political and cultural dominance from one people to another, it nevertheless reminds one of the need to continue to care for, about and with others regarding the flourishing of humanity. And, it is with the latter in mind, that a philosophy of higher education in Africa will achieve much in the quest to advance humaneness, justice and care.

References

Loizou, A. (2018). *Time, embodiment, and the self.* London: Routledge.
Metz, T. (2018). An African theory of the point of higher education: Communion as an alternative to autonomy, truth, and citizenship. In A. Stoller & E. Kramer (Eds.), *Toward a philosophy of higher education: Contemporary philosophical proposals for the university* (pp. 161–186). New York: Palgrave Macmillan.
Puerta Vilchez, J. M. (2010). *Reading the Alhambra: A visual guide to the Alhambra through its inscriptions.* Granada, Spain: The Alhambra and Generalife Trust & EDILUX.
Stoller, A., & Kramer, E. (Eds.). (2018). *Toward a philosophy of higher education: Contemporary philosophical proposals for the university.* New York: Palgrave Macmillan.

Waghid, Y. (2014). *African philosophy of education reconsidered: On being human.* London: Routledge.

Waghid, Y., Waghid, F., & Waghid, Z. (2018). *Rupturing African philosophy on teaching and learning: Ubuntu justice and education.* New York: Palgrave Macmillan.

13

Towards a Re-imagined Notion of University Education: In Defence of a Reconstituted Ethics of Care

Introduction

In this chapter, we argue that women on the African continent experience moments of internal exclusion in HEIs. Although women are statistically represented – attaining external inclusion in minimal ways – they remain subjected to internal exclusion on the grounds that their contributions are evidently unsubstantive. Through a conceptual analysis of women's experiences of African higher education, this chapter reveals that internal exclusion can be attributed to a gendered view of equality, mostly generated in people's social, political and cultural practices. We contend that an equalisation of voice rather than gender may possibly disrupt the status quo and undermine the debilitating conditions that perpetuate women's internal exclusion on the continent. By examining the implications of a reconstituted ethics of care for university education, this chapter offers some ways in which exclusionary practices can be remedied. We contend that, if higher education in Africa (university education) were to halt the dilemma of internal exclusion and move towards

With Rachel Ndinelao Shanyanana, University of Namibia, Namibia

engendering a reconstituted ethics of care, then it stands an authentic chance of cultivating compassionate, imaginative and responsible citizens who can reason, not only for themselves, but for humanity as well.

Towards Inclusion and Gender Equality in African Higher Education

African countries have experienced a long period of colonialism imposed by most prominent Western colonial powers such as France, Belgium, Britain, Germany and Portugal, to mention just a few. Upon liberation, the assumption was that HEIs in these countries would be accessible to all people, irrespective of gender, race, status, ethnicity or religion – a way of engendering inclusion. The idea of liberation in Africa was influenced extensively by the Brazilian philosopher, Paulo Freire's (2004) liberatory perspectives on education, which entailed setting one free from all forms of domination and dependence. For this reason, different democratic initiatives were spearheaded by the World Declarations and the United Nations Millennium Development Goals (MDGs) to promote a democratic society in which all people live equally and justly. In 2000, the United Nations promulgated the MDGs, with the aim of achieving the following eight fundamental goals:

- eradicate poverty and hunger;
- achieve universal primary education;
- promote gender equality and empower women;
- reduce child mortality;
- improve maternal health;
- combat HIV and AIDS, malaria and other diseases;
- ensure environmental sustainability; and
- develop a global partnership for development by 2015 (United Nations MDGs, 2005: v).

Having said that, the idea of gender equality and women's empowerment is at the heart of the MDGs, to which many African nations are signatories. Gender equality and women's empowerment demand that each designated country should achieve 50% gender equality by 2015.

In this regard, African countries introduced the New Partnership for African Development (NEPAD, 2002), a project with a vision to achieve the MDGs at all levels of society, especially in the area of women's inclusion and gender equality in all educational institutions in order to foster social and economic development. Undoubtedly, the fundamental goal is to alleviate social exclusion and marginalisation to advance women's legitimate inclusion at all levels. Inclusion and gender equality in Africa surfaced as a global and local agenda in higher education at the World Conference on Higher Education in Paris in 1998 (UNESCO, 1998). This concern was twofold, namely women's lower enrolments in higher education to date, and the absence of the gender dimension in the HE curriculum. That concern gave birth to the introduction of affirmative action (AA), which was promulgated to promote the inclusion of women in higher education. Morley (2004) refers to AA as a policy adopted by many African countries to engender gender equality and inclusion of more women at all levels of society, especially in higher education.

However, Morley's study in four Commonwealth HEIs indicates that AA programmes could make women passive and dependent:

> [I]t will not work out that way, because in spite of doing everything for the female and thinking things will work out that way, the female has to be independent to some certain level and if she gets to a place where everything is being done for her, the product at the end of the day will not be worth it. So, they have to really think about it, yes, help us, but don't go too far. (Morley, 2004: 18)

At face value, creating a policy merely for women's access to university education in Africa, without hearing their voices, does not indicate genuine inclusion, considering that in the cultural background of many of the women, only men are permitted in the public space. Arising from the above, one could argue that, although much effort has been expended on the issue of inclusion, there remains a crisis of exclusion on the continent. One may concede that the impetus for an inclusive democratic society is driven by various international conventions and policies that coerce African institutions, especially higher education to create a space for the marginalised and excluded groups.

Dunne and Pendlebury (2003: 208) argue that higher education (specifically university education) is required to play the role of cultivating special dimensions of character and special virtues that are necessary for the sustainability of a democratic regime. They also argue that public schools (including higher education) constitute the best arenas for the promotion of democratic virtues, such as inclusion. Consequently, if public schools are not democratic, this situation is less likely to exist in other institutions of society. It can be conceived that the practices of higher education ought to operate effectively if such practices are conducted within an inclusive and democratic environment in which everyone's interest is considered in HE practices, irrespective of colour, race and gender. Likewise, Gutmann and Thompson (2004: 35) affirm that the education system is one of the central places in any democracy where the preparation for future free and equal citizens can appropriately be done. That being said, since most African states are democratic nations, HEIs that are considered hubs of knowledge ought to cultivate a democratic citizenry that could not only compete in the world market economy, but also assist in addressing local predicaments on the continent. Thus, the mission of the public university should be to educate students to acquire knowledge and skills that would enable them to engage in debate and offer possible solutions to burning issues facing the continent today.

Nevertheless, studies have shown that women have been and still are being excluded from African higher education (AHE) (Assié-Lumumba, 2007; Kiamba, 2008; Kwesiga, 2002: 152). Despite the fact that different conferences and studies have proposed ways of inclusion, such as MDGs projects that aim to address exclusion and gender inequality, the dilemma remains prevalent on the continent. Such an impasse of inclusion may thwart the continent's envisaged MDG goal of attaining 50% women representation and gender equality by 2015 to 2020. In my view, although HEIs – particularly universities – occupy an integral part of a democratic society in which future free and equal citizens ought to be nurtured; it would not be unreasonable to infer that substantive inclusion has been achieved. With this in mind, before substantiating our claim for women exclusion in Africa, it is necessary to explore what inclusion entails.

Internal Exclusion as an Impasse in University Education

In a literal sense, inclusion means involving others or inviting them to participate in doing something in public. A preliminary understanding of the concept of inclusion is recognised as a norm for democratic society, including the HE community (Young, 2000: 23–25). The idea of inclusion in decision-making plays a central role in democratic discourses and society in which everyone ought to be included in public deliberative engagement. The inclusive processes of communication ought to be marked by people's disposition to be accountable to others and to make deliberation open to the public, making it accessible for it to count as normatively legitimate (Young, 2000: 13). This approach envisages that decisions on ways to address and promote inclusive democratic institutions such as HE bodies are legitimate. The question is whether a legitimate public HE system be sustained in Africa if women and other groups are excluded. Young (2000) argues that justified inclusion can only happen when all stakeholders are included in the process, which needs to take place irrespective of their gender and other differences. This model promotes the idea that each person has the right to be included and treated as important in the dialogues and decision-making processes from which their voices and interests were previously excluded.

Paradoxically, Young (2000) states that, while mechanisms are hastened to include all stakeholders, new forms of exclusion come into play, i.e. exclusion is intrinsic within inclusive democratic processes. This view shows that a more nuanced understanding of inclusion should be one that contends with forms of exclusion in a subtle way. In other words, inclusion could be inclusive and simultaneously, exclusive. A notion of inclusion as argued for by Young (2000) presumes that women's presence in AHEIs will be far more inclusive than a reliance on mere statistics and percentages if they are substantively included on the grounds of their contributions. That is, their inclusion would be substantive rather than just statistically viable. Moreover, those included also experience various forms of exclusion. This view reinforces our argument that post-colonial AHE excludes women, in spite of various mechanisms for promoting their inclusion. Even though inclusion and equality are fundamental to facilitating public deliberation for a functional and inclusive democratic society, exclusion is inherent within inclusion, as access of women to higher education becomes apparent while, at the same time, their voices are not considered in deliberations and decision-making.

On the concept of exclusion inherent within inclusion, Young (2000: 52–53) delineates two approaches – internal exclusion and external exclusion. The first approach involves individuals or groups being formally represented in social institutions, but being excluded from the discussion and decision-making process by means of a specific style of expression, where the use of language is difficult to understand, and the dismissal of the participation of some people is regarded as being out of order. The second approach occurs when some members are kept out of a democratic community and its debates or decision-making processes, that is, such people (e.g. women) are not involved in a community of engagement and in public discourses due to their status in society (Young, 2000: 52–53). Higher education seems to advance external exclusion, as it denies women's access and contributions to HE practices. An example of external exclusion is found where women are not admitted to HEIs at all, while the few with access to higher education, are internally excluded by being denied space to contribute to debates or decision-making processes. Teferra and Altbach (2004: 21) point out that the challenges experienced by female students include a lack of access to higher education as well as the problem of gender inequality amongst students and academic staff in many African universities.

Exemplifying external exclusion, a study of 32 universities in 16 African countries showed that a large proportion of university dropouts comprised female students (Leathwood & Read, 2009: 3). This implies that women are not only underrepresented numerically, but they are also at a higher risk of non-completion and dropping out. With many student groups still underrepresented, higher education continues to be criticised for being elite-based rather than open for the masses. The idea that higher education limits women's equal access to its practices seems to say that there is no space for women; thus, confirming a kind of exclusion. A study conducted by the London Institute of Education (2005: 10) shows that the percentage of female enrolment in higher education in Africa was low at the time. Nigeria had 39.9%, Tanzania 24% and Uganda 34%, while Lesotho 50% and South Africa were the only countries at the time with 53% female enrolment. Many of the female students in HEIs are clustered at the undergraduate level, and more are studying for certificates and diplomas, while fewer females are found at the master's and doctoral levels. It is evident that women are not only under-represented as students at universities, but also as staff members. Undeniably, such a selection of data on higher education on the continent reveals a sizeable gender gap, the cause of which needs to be interrogated.

From the number of women appointed as heads of HEIs – as rectors, vice-rectors, chancellors and deans of faculties – it is evident that universities in Africa promote women's exclusion and gender inequality in staff membership. Onokala and Onah (1998: 10–12) revealed that, at the time, African universities had produced at least five female vice-chancellors from different disciplines. It is observed that African universities in the twenty-first century need to strive to become places where the pursuit of knowledge is indeed freely and equally available to all citizens, irrespective of age, religion, sex and race. A research study conducted by the London Institute of Education (2005: 5) found that, at the time, there was also a sizeable gender gap in staff employment, particularly at higher decision-making levels. At the time, out of the four Commonwealth African universities examined, the percentages of women at the level of professor, associate professor and senior lecturer were decidedly lower than those of men. Even at the lowest level of academic opportunities, such as assistant lecturers, the percentage was surprisingly low, indicating that women were deprived of contributions as role models and mentors in higher education. Statistics of positions of professor held by women at the four universities showed that, at the time, Ibadan University had 12.5%, the University of Cape Town 7%, Dar es Salam University 5.2%, and Makerere University 6.1%. Positions of associate professor held by women constituted 17% in Cape Town, 14.8% in Dar es Salam, and 20% in Makerere (London Institute of Education, 2005: 5).

In addition, statistics of women as rectors, vice-chancellors, deputy chancellors, registrars, executive directors and deans of faculties showed that, in 2006, in terms of the overall gender proportion of the 92 African universities, only four countries attained 30%, namely Lesotho, Mauritius,

Namibia and Swaziland. Countries such as South Africa, Mozambique, Uganda and Botswana had 28%, while the rest had between 0 and 24% representation of women (HERS-SA, 2008: 2). The foregoing statistics are indicative of women's exclusion and gender inequality in the early years of this century, which, at the time, seemed to prevail not only in higher education, but also at other levels of society. The point is that women were externally included in minimal ways, but not substantively included. The concept of gender equality is viewed by King and Mason (2001: 34–35) in terms of equality under law and equality of opportunity, including equality of access to higher education, knowledge production and human capital as well as other productive resources, and equality of rewards for work and equality of voice. It seems that women as students and staff members did not have enough access to and experience in AHE at the time. According to Assié-Lumumba (2007: 472), there is evidence of a severe lack of female access to higher education. It is stated that no African country has achieved the goal of universal primary education (Assié-Lumumba, 2007), much less the goal of ensuring access to HE for women. We contend that, in Africa, exclusion and gender inequality are underlying factors that cause a lack of access of women to higher education as both students and staff members.

On the notion of access, Morrow (2007: 39) identifies two types, formal access and epistemological access. Formal access deals with admission to HEIs in terms of the number of students, whereas epistemological access entails how many institutions provide access to the goods they distribute to those it formally admits, i.e. the knowledge shared system. For instance, formal access takes place when more women (as students or staff members) are given special entry to higher education, but epistemological access is enabled when women who gained formal access to higher education are offered spaces to share their knowledge by means of research outputs at conferences and in publications, and to make contributions to policy changes. Morrow (2007: 39) consequently rightly notes that, if we promise our students (in this case, women) spaces in higher education by offering them formal access, but break our promise by not offering them adequate epistemological access, we not only betray their personal aspirations, but also undermine some of the central ideals of higher education. The point is that women are excluded; therefore, they lack formal and epistemological access.

In a sense, higher education offers the means through which women and other historically disadvantaged groups can attain positions of leadership and increase their economic welfare, thereby having a long-term influence on the overall productivity and the idea of equal opportunity (Adetude & Akensina, 2008: 339). It is apparent that women appear not only to be denied their rights as equal human beings, but their opportunities are curtailed and their voices are silenced. This may be related to discriminatory activities against them in higher education as both students and staff members. This brings us to the argument that by denying women both formal and epistemological access (a way of exclusion), they are deprived of opportunities in the institutions that would have contributed considerably more to their upliftment, empowerment and self-esteem. They would also have been equipped with cognitive ability, become more critical and be afforded critical tools to address societal problems, all things that higher education ought to do. Hence, we argue that the bleak situation of the exclusion of women from higher education in Africa requires collective and concerted efforts that engender inclusive and equal institutions if credible knowledge production and development are to be advanced and protected.

In relation to internal exclusion, we argue that, although women as students and staff members are externally included, there is evidence of internal exclusion in AHE. The problem of justifying internal exclusion is that, scientifically, one may not identify this form of exclusion. However, a gaze on women's narratives and shared stories reveals it nonetheless. As Young (2000) postulates, exclusion is inherent within inclusion. As soon as one claims to be included – in this case, based on statistics – one continues to experience other forms of exclusion, such as vicious discrimination and prejudicial remarks that provoke exclusion. Epitomising the evidence of women's experiences of internal exclusion, Maürtin-Cairncross (2013: 1) posits that women have entered the academic arena only relatively recently, and the male-dominated enterprise in academe remains evident. Men, Cairncross (2013: 1) avers, continue to dominate senior positions, as women struggle to establish themselves within the 'centre' of the academe. Based on Maürtin-Cairncross's study conducted in South Africa, women experience some sense of invisibility and exclusion within their workplaces. Different academic respondents in her study stated:

> Women are made to feel invisible[;] one is often called to meetings and informed of decisions that were made. When challenging these decisions, you are "allowed" to speak but at the end of your discussion, the initial decision is reiterated as if you had not spoken at all. That is the reason that some women become aggressive....they want to be heard; they want their opinions to be taken seriously. When they react in this way, they are labelled emotional.... So what does one do [?] I have taken to remain[ing] silent ... (Respondent 1, higher education executive). (Maürtin-Cairncross, 2013: 1)

> The work climate females experience in a very covert way excludes women from the real decision making... They [the men] have a camaraderie which excludes women, in the real sense. Women are listened to, without taking their points seriously. [Men's] importance and being busy becomes an excuse for hoarding information and creating a sense of power that hides their inefficiencies. (Respondent 2, higher education executive)

> [B]eing overlooked because of perceptions about you (age, EI [emotional intelligence], intelligence not being taken seriously by the senior managers and being overlooked for the work you deliver on in favour of someone else ...). (Respondent 5, director)

From the above, we deduce that women, especially those in senior positions, often feel excluded from decision-making because their presence and ideas are often ignored. Furthermore, some respondents identified their exclusion as being inculcated by the limited number of women in senior positions in higher education, which means that the few women's voices in such decision-making do not have an influence in male-dominated institutions (Maürtin-Cairncross, 2013: 1):

> There are not many women role models or people who have occupied similar positions from whom I can learn. It is my perception that those who are out there are extremely busy or I do not know about them. There is definitely no "old/experienced girls club" and again it is my opinion that women do not form groups who call on each other for support. (Respondent 7, director)

> [There is a] lack of a critical mass of women in leadership positions, leading to isolation, which in turn often means that women do not have the confi-

dence or support to take on styles and approaches different [than those of] male colleagues. (Respondent 8, executive member, women's network)

I also found that all departments/areas of the institution were not going to assist me at the initial phases. They did not see it as "their business" – probably because people did not understand. Perhaps fear of change also has a great impact. (Respondent 9, director)

Noticeably, women's experiences demonstrate that, when they feel invisible and excluded, especially when they are only a few in senior positions where they are expected to influence decisions and policymaking, they consequently become afraid to act with confidence. The following quotations reflect some of these sentiments (Maürtin-Cairncross, 2013: 1):

Lack of confidence on the part of many women [keeps them from being] bold and stand[ing] up for themselves. (Respondent 5, director)

Male counterparts … are driven by a fear that they may lose power and therefore they do not share it. They do self-esteem-lowering things – ignore people… [implying] I am busier than you and therefore I can give you only limited time and space! Women's need to be made to feel valued is never addressed. Building self-esteem…you have to find these things for yourself and spend energy on "bouncing back" and keeping your own power as they will take it away from you and make you feel inferior; if you are not working from an inner center of strength you are doomed. (Respondent 2, higher education executive)

The foregoing experiences in higher education illustrate how people without self-confidence could find it difficult to assert their voices as equal agents and stand up for their arguments, on the one hand, largely because of the fact that there are few women representatives in senior positions. On the other hand, the challenge faced is due to women's resistance to support one another's standpoints, as well as their promotion. We agree with Maürtin-Cairncross (2013: 2) that, even though the 'dominant social groups often control the channels of communication, reinforcing women's subordinate status, when academic women do not challenge dominant institutional cultures, they may tacitly accept subordinate status'.

This suggests that only when women have the confidence to challenge these exclusionary attitudes and practices by demanding their equal space might their ideas possibly be taken into consideration as a way of attaining internal inclusion. The point is that internal exclusion is implicit, evident only as expressed in women's experiences, which makes it difficult for it to be revealed by looking at statistics on the numbers of women and men. Our argument is extended by UNESCO-UIS (2010: 68–71), which maintains:

> We should start by considering what the data do not reveal. The fact that a rising number of women are pursuing higher education does not mean that there are fewer opportunities for men. The growth in female enrolment partly reflects the changing values and attitudes related to the roles and aspirations of women in society that are the legacy of social change and feminist movements which emerged globally in the 1960s and 1970s.

Thus, what we find troubling is that the current discourse, which champions access as inclusion, appears to be surface rather than substantive inclusion. Although most of these women's experiences are extracted from South Africa, we argue that such forms of exclusion are evident in different countries on the continent. A study of two universities, one in Cape Coast, Ghana and the other in Dar es Salaam, Tanzania, on the crisis of widening participation in public higher education, revealed that, although policies are prevalent, 'poorer and mature students were still absent from higher education' (Morley, 2012: 21). Although such universities have stipulated quotas for female students, especially those from disadvantaged groups, there are no monitoring systems to show that such students actually participate in programmes and complete their studies. Morley observes that two hundred students from disadvantaged backgrounds (particularly women) shared their unsatisfactory experiences in primary, secondary and higher education. Morley noted that students from diverse backgrounds, including under-represented groups (women, mature students, low socio-economic status, and people with disabilities) often experience hardship in their HE encounters (Morley, 2012: 22).

Furthermore, the access by and participation of female students from poor socio-economic backgrounds depend on loans and bursaries, while mature women share the stress of earning, as well as of extended family responsibilities. Those with disabilities have no provision for accessing HEIs, which indicates that exclusion from higher education could be experienced differently by women from diverse backgrounds and conditions. Sharing their experiences of higher education, some students acknowledged support from a number of caring individuals working in higher education, such as lecturers, counsellors and advisors (Morley, 2012: 22). Clearly, some students appreciate the support and care provided by staff members to enable them to excel. This is interesting to note, as it suggests that higher education might turn into a caring public institution if staff members practise some form of care. However, the evidence suggests that forms of exclusion are perpetuated in higher education, specifically in relation to disadvantaged groups, including women.

Augmenting subtle forms of internal exclusion in AHE as expressed in different studies (such as Maürtin-Cairncross, 2013; Morley, 2012), we draw from various engagements with female students during postgraduate pedagogical deliberations and seminars at Stellenbosch University between 2013 and 2014. Amongst them were students from a number of African countries, namely South Africa, Lesotho, Zimbabwe, Mozambique, Kenya, Uganda and Nigeria, who shared their experiences of internal exclusion in higher education. For instance, one of these students indicated that internal exclusion emanates from a number of issues: in her case, a lack of confidence to engage in deliberation due to her lack of proficiency in English. She preferred to speak to the lecturer or presenter after the seminar, rather than to engage with them in public. She acknowledged that she often had ideas, but to air them in public became a fearful exercise. This student, like others, felt that few female students who engage in deliberations are comfortable and certain of what they are saying. Another student agreed that fear of airing an idea that might be dismissed, and one's inability to offer an argument and defend it, comprised another issue.

In similar engagements, some students identified insensitive comments from other women, especially regarding when one will give birth. In her words, 'I get irritated by such comments and I can't understand why my study is seen as not important till I produce a baby.' Such remarks left her with doubt about whether she should have babies or focus on her studies first, which provoked a sense of insecurity in the presence of colleagues with babies. Another issue shared by some married women was related to questions about whether their husbands helped them or wrote the work for them. Some single women's educational relationships with male lecturers are often questioned. This is related to what Wagner-Martin (1994: 21) refers to as 'the trap of the stereotype', where she argues that the first question that 'still asks of any women is whose daughter [wife or student] she is … The traditions of both patriarchy and heterosexuality are confirmed'. From the above experiences, we argue that internal exclusion is provoked by numerous issues, such as poor language proficiency, fear of intimidation, discomfort about speaking in public, lack of confidence and inability to defend one's argument, as well as sexist or prejudicial remarks about giving birth, and connecting a women's work either to a husband or female supervisor. We then contend that, if universities in Africa will not take the issue of internal exclusion seriously, then legitimate transformation will remain a dream. Women's physical representation in AHE as a strategy for mitigating external exclusion is an indisputable achievement. However, we are concerned about the absence of women's voices in democratic processes and decision-making – a disconcerting encounter of women's internal exclusion in higher education in Africa. Given the above predicament, in the next section, we show how gender as a yardstick to equality inhibits internal inclusion.

Transcending a Gender-Based Inclusion Towards Equalisation of Voice

Regarding gender, Butler (1990: 2–5) shows the limits of reflexivity in thinking about the self beyond the dichotomy of sex and gender. In her view, the distinction between sex and gender seems to be increasingly unstable, since gender is radically independent of sex and is a 'free-floating artifice' (Butler, 1990: 7, 22). This implies that gender identifies those things that do not conform to the system of 'compulsory and naturalized heterosexuality', and divulges how gender norms are socially instituted and maintained. Profoundly, Butler's argument prompts us to explore an appropriate means of understanding equality further, besides seeing it from the position of gender, which is constructed with women and men in mind and does not account for those who fall outside the dichotomy. Subsequently, 'gender is a process which has neither origin nor end, it is something that we do rather than we are' (Butler, 1990: 128–129). We found this understanding of gender compelling, particularly the idea that being a woman or a man is something that is constructed. Conversely, the challenge resulting from the identification of gender based on biological differences between women and men is that the categorisation leads to constructed discourse with the intention of recreating hegemonic paradigms and perpetuating today's power relations – including in social institutions such as AHE (Butler, 1990: 182–185; Tamale, 2011). In this respect, defining women and men as universal categories disguises the interests such definition serves. As a result, anything that is defined as natural or universal should be studied critically. We would agree, therefore, that gender should not only be approached based on the categories of man and woman, but also on the different social relations that prevail among them.

Thus, if AHE has embodied this perspective of gender categorisation, as seems to be the case, the possibility of achieving equality is limited. We are challenged to envisage equality differently, not presuming that the conception of inclusion and gender equality in postcolonial AHE leads to democracy. With Butler's (1990) gender perspective, one is impelled to investigate what democratic higher education ought to be, since equality based on gender poses more danger for internal inclusion in AHE. The fact that the justification of equality continues to be approached on the basis of the number of female (or male) students and staff members of higher institutions, those who are outside the gender categorisation (women or men) will obviously be excluded. In that case, the democratic deliberations will end up ignoring their presence and continue to exclude them. Butler (1990) sees gender categorisation within a dominant ideology of heterosexuality as a social construct in which every person can decide what he or she wants to become. Like Butler, some African scholars, namely Tamale (2011), Imam (1997: 2) and Obi (2003) echo that gender is essentially a social construct and largely denotes the social and historical constructions of masculine and feminine roles. In addition, the entire range of institutions, values and practices are inherently built to sustain deepen and, certainly, undermine it. Obi (2003: 6) highlights that there is nothing natural about gender roles and that they could be static or dynamic, based on the equilibrium of social forces and the influence of factors of history, culture, power and production. In this section, we work in consonance with Obi's assertion that the reality of male domination over female subordination is reproduced, thereby intensifying its salience to social mobilisation. This implies that the analysis of gender 'invariably focuses on women, and the ways the architecture of social power tend to subordinate the female to male power' (Obi, 2003: 6).

Gender relations are therefore engaged as social constructs that reflect the dominant power relationships among people. The systematic patterns of internal exclusion and the effect of other forms of relationships with other groups cannot be ignored. This is because different people experience internal exclusion differently, based on their level of confidence and their ability to disrupt the power relationships confronting them. The point is that no one should rely on gender as a standard or an approach to engender internal inclusion, considering the fact that it is socially constructed. As we argued earlier, gendered roles lead women to be relegated to specific fields, courses, jobs and positions that correlate with their assigned or socially constructed roles. In this way, women may continue to encounter internal exclusion instigated by exclusionary practices and structures. And this will jeopardise the AHE agenda, namely to attain substantive inclusion. We concur that gender categorisation could further exacerbate internal exclusion when used as yardstick for inclusion. In other words, gauging inclusion on the ground of gender is an inadequate approach and may not help Africa to address exclusion, particularly internal exclusion, which is rampant in HEIs. The interrelatedness of the constitutive elements should consider the dilemma of representation in universities and the dynamic of gender categorisation, which perceives women's voice and those outside the gender category as not human enough to be considered. We therefore call for equality of voice as a means to inclusion beyond gender.

Intellectual Equality Through an Assertion of Voice

Here, we draw on Jacques Rancière's idea (1992: 41; 101) of equal intelligences founded on two principles, namely 'everyone is of equal intelligence', and 'everyone's similarity, and everyone's ability to voluntary thinking'. The points emanating from the emancipatory method of teaching are that everyone has similar intelligence, everyone is able to teach him- or herself, and everything is everything, which means 'all power of the language is in the totality of a book' (Rancière, 1992: 26). For Rancière, human beings are equal in terms of their intelligence, which we find vibrant in influencing caring relationships between an educator and student as they engage in pedagogical encounters. In this respect, taking caring in the same manner, the internally excluded groups are to be recognised based on their intellectual equality, which will not only instil in them critical thinking skills, but also announce their presence via a voice. The point is that, since all people can think, we evaluate people's attainment of equality on the basis of people's voice rather than gender, as has always been the case. In our view, equalisation of voice is a plausible approach to disrupt internal exclusion.

In Rancière's (1999) view, inclusion signifies a framework of thinking about equality that describes a way to act out, rather than distribute, equality. We agree that equality of voice embodies a process whereby individuals act on their own behalf, rather than being represented by others. The idea of acting on their own behalf ties in very well with an inclusive higher education, in which women, like other members, engage in educational deliberations and demand their deliberative spaces. Nonetheless, when people are being represented, the representatives act in support of others for the purpose of achieving equality on the assumption that they are acting on behalf of others, that is the marginalised groups (women, the disabled and the poor) who are incapable of asserting their own equality. For us, this idea of being represented is rather incapacitating and non-emancipatory, since the voices of the excluded will remain on the margin. Rancière (1999: 33) succinctly points out:

> [E]quality is not a given that politics presses into service, an essence embodied in the law or a goal politics sets itself the task of attaining; it is a mere assumption that needs to be discerned within the practices implementing it.

This simply means that equality cannot be achieved only when those who are deprived of it receive it through others, but also when they engage in educational deliberations in their own capacity. In other words, when women are receiving equality it would still mean that others must give it to them, which eschew their agency as equal citizens. In concurrence with Rancière (1999: 30), equality is a way of disrupting and attaining justice, and that is what people (women) are entitled to expect from the state or social institutions (higher education) in which they happen to find themselves.

Attaining equality is based on how people ought to act and what they do while claiming their equality – even in AHE arrangements. Rancière argues that equality is not a principle of receptivity or passivity – attained by being visible in AHE without making any meaningful contribution. Rather, it is a principle of activity. We find Rancière's view of people (women) engaging in a particular activity to demand equality, rather than waiting as passive recipients of what is being distributed to them, quite compelling. Women, and in fact all categories of people, ought to be included as a way of claiming their equality with their voice. This approach has the potential to engender equality in higher education, as it could empower and change the position of women, enabling them to air their voices like their male counterparts. Thus, only when AHE creates an enabling atmosphere in which all voices are heard will equality be achieved. Women should not expect to receive equality as passive objects and to be recipients of services; they need to demand what is rightfully theirs through vigorous inclusion. In this way, an appropriate and active form of equality in AHE would be engendered.

The potential question is how women and other excluded groups may demand their inclusion in post-colonial democratic institutions such as AHE. Responding to the query whether those who lack capacity and confidence, particularly African women, might possibly be able to act and claim their equality, Rancière (1992: 46) posits that equality can be acted out based on the equality of intelligence. To him, equality of intelligence does not imply that students have the capability to score the same marks or grades; rather, it implies equality of intelligence on a standard basis. In other words, intellectual skills may vary from one person to another, but we are equally capable of using those skills to communicate, to discuss, to make decisions, and to take account of the world around us. Hence, to promote 'equalisation of voice', AHE ought to nurture in all people, irrespective of their gender, some sense of assertiveness, which may enable women to engage in debates and offer their reasons with confidence. At the same time, there is a need to cultivate the ability to listen, with attentive listening to all members of an educational community as a way of promoting internal inclusion. The above view suggests that human beings (men and women) possess equal intelligence and rights to voice; it is inescapable for inclusion and equality to move beyond gender. Rather, educational discourses should consider inclusion based on 'equalisation of voice'. In terms of voice, people will listen to the standpoints of others, without considering which gender or group is making the claim. The standard will be to judge whether an act makes sense or not. Subsequently, to attain the level where people utter a voice and listen attentively, university education needs to educate citizens with such attributes.

Our contention is that, if all human beings indeed have similar intellectual skills, then institutions and educators need to create an environment in which all students could unleash their potential and exercise attentive listening in their effort to attain equality. In our view, 'equalisation of voice' is an ideal approach to the inclusion not only of women, but of other excluded groups, such as homosexuals. Furthermore, a Rancièrean framework of equality as disruption through a voice is remarkable and could be used as a benchmark for internal inclusion. This means that being attentive is to be assertive and to disrupt the conversation. In other words, this rich conception offers a sufficient, reconstructed framework that moves beyond an inclusion based on gender, to one that recognises human voice in an inclusive democratic higher education in Africa, where many women and other marginalised groups aspire to experience humanity. It is in this light that we utilise Rancière's (1992) idea of equal intelligence, which epitomises how all people need to be viewed as equal human beings by the assertion of their voice, which may disrupt the exclusionary practices in AHE. Yet, for university education to engender inclusion through equalisation of voice, there is a need for a paradigm shift – which is a reconstituted ethics of care.

Caring as a Human Capacity: Engendering a Reconstituted Ethics of Care

Already, I have alluded to the fact that this work builds on Noddings's (1984) idea of care. This section aims to extend Noddings's (1984) conception of caring as a relational act between the carer and cared-for by reconstituting an ethics of care that transcends the gender divide and may disrupt the internal exclusion that pervades AHE. In terms of our choice of Noddings's caring approach, we acknowledge that an ethics of care is not comprehensive and there are other approaches to address exclusion like Slote's (2007) work on care and compassion. However, we find the ideas of Noddings on caring (if reconstituted) more feasible in engendering internal inclusion. Noddings (1992) encourages educators to practise caring as a perfect form for education and schooling. Her viewpoint is that, when students are cared for, they can learn to care for themselves, for others (those known to them and those unknown), and for plants, animals and ideas (Noddings, 1992: 174–175). To put it succinctly, our strangeness or differences within AHE should not prevent us from caring for each other, especially those in the excluded groups. We echo her viewpoint that if we cannot have caring relationships with those we do not know personally, then our moral relationships with them demand that it would be wrong not to help people in a distant country who are victims of famine, HIV and AIDS, rape, sexual harassment and other forms of marginalisation, including internal exclusion encountered by women in AHE.

To give meaning to a potential caring approach, we defend Rancière's (1992) idea of equalisation of voice as a plausible approach to internal inclusion. The equalisation of voice framework recognises that all people (females or males) have equal intelligence. Thus, they require exercising their rights through assertion of voice as a way of disrupting the status quo and exclusionary patterns in AHE to transcend the gender divide. We defend Rancière's (1992) equalisation of voice as a disruption of the exclusionary relationships that proliferate internal exclusion in AHE. In essence, we contend that caring is a human capacity and can be expressed by all human beings, irrespective of their gender, class or other differences. Central questions that impel this exploration are:

- What would human relations actually look like when they are not distinguished on a gender basis?
- What constitutes a reconstituted ethics of care that could engender equalisation of voice?

As a response to this interrogation, we proceed to explore how a caring relationship that evokes equalisation of voice can be enacted. The first facet that could evoke equalisation of voice towards internal inclusion is compassionate imagining.

Caring as Compassionate Imagining

The idea of compassionate imagining is derived from Nussbaum's (2001) call for emotion, namely compassion, to embrace democratic deliberation. In her view, compassion entails that people — in this case, the carer and cared-for — recognise one another's vulnerabilities and misfortunes. For her, compassion is a significant emotion to cultivate when preparing people to engage in deliberation and just action, in public as well as in private affairs (Nussbaum, 2001: 299). Likewise, we concur with Nussbaum (2001) that enacting caring towards students requires compassionate respect as a guiding act in AHE deliberations. To her, emotional impetus should underlie democratic deliberation in order to treat students justly and humanely, which is treating them with compassion. The point is that the caring educator and caring act should consider the students' limitations, especially those from disadvantaged backgrounds – be these educational, social, financial or intellectual.

Needless to say, some students might find it challenging to engage in a provocative engagement that may reinforce subordination and silence of the excluded group. As argued elsewhere, most women from African societies are reared not to speak in the same manner as their male counterparts (Shanyanana, 2011). Therefore, in considering the foregoing view of their limitations, engaging with an inducement of provocation might help the excluded groups to articulate their views and develop reasoning abilities. Thus, caring relationships need to consider such misfortunes as the carer strives to inculcate people's rational potentialities. It is for this reason that the emotion of compassion becomes an imperative constituent for acting with care and deliberating about such matters, since compassion not only prompts in people an awareness of the misfortune or suffering of others, but also 'pushes the boundaries of the self' outward by focusing one's attention on the suffering of others (Nussbaum, 2001: 299). We hold, that in order to act in a caring manner, the carer needs to have regard for the other person, in other words, being compassionate towards the cared-for.

In answering the question how and why human beings ought to become compassionate, Nussbaum (2001) conceptualises compassion as an agonising emotional judgement that comprises two cognitive requirements. The first requirement demands that there should be a belief or appraisal that the suffering of others is serious and not trivial, and that the cared-for student, like other citizens, does not deserve to suffer. The second requirement is that there is a belief that the possibilities of the person (carer) who experiences emotion are similar to those of the sufferer (cared-for). Looking at the two requirements of compassionate emotion, we proceed to show how the cared-for students and carer educator ought to apply compassion to rational deliberative engagement, which concomitantly enacts caring, that is being compassionate, with a concern to be just and humane towards others in AHE. We reckon that one needs to be compassionate in the caring relationship by recognising that the misfortune, i.e. the internal exclusion and limited rationality, is not of their fault; hence, the need to act to address it. The point we are making is that compassion can be expressed to all people suffering either through their own fault or otherwise. However, this chapter centres on the internally excluded due to a myriad of forms of injustice experienced.

The point Nussbaum (2001: 317) makes is that human beings need to be compassionate by recognising that those who experience misfortune, in this case the excluded groups, do not do so due to their own fault, but that their plight needs to be addressed. On the other hand, compassion can be enacted if one acknowledges a caring relationship as a form of community between the carer and cared-for, particularly understanding what it means for one to experience vulnerabilities similar to those of the victim. In the words of Nussbaum (2001: 317):

> [One] will learn compassion best if he [she] begins by focusing on their sufferings … [I]n order for compassion to be present, the person must consider the suffering of another as a significant part of his or her own scheme of goals and ends. She must take that person's ill as affecting her own flourishing. In effect, she must make herself vulnerable in the person of another.

This recognition of one's vulnerability requires of the caring educator to have a deeper understanding of what it feels like to be internally excluded from the democratic processes of which one is said to be a part. In essence, the caring educator should not only imagine the inabilities and vulnerabilities of the cared-for, but should rather act by taking responsible risks to include the excluded.

Caring as Taking Responsibility

The idea of acknowledging humanity by taking responsibility is central to a reconstituted ethics of care if those internally excluded are to assert their voice and offer justifiable reasons as equal citizens. Cavell (1979) calls for acknowledging humanity, which entails showing respect for people's dignity as human beings. According to Cavell (1979: 438, 440), acknowledging humanity 'in Other and oneself' means that one sees yourself through the Other – that makes the Other a mirror that casts one's image towards yourself, and suggests that there is some interconnectedness between the Other and yourself. Being a mirror image of the other in Cavellian terms requires one to be 'answerable for what happens to them', that is, to enact one's responsibility towards them. In this sense, the Other – the actual Other as well as the Other in oneself – confronts the self and therefore s/he is turned back upon his or her own self; therefore, the Other is not simply the friend, but becomes the teacher, the possibility of self-transcendence. The ability of the self to move beyond those known to us is central to Cavell's argument that 'the Other is like oneself, that whatever one can know about the other one first has to find in oneself and then read into the other … [that is to] conceive the other from the other's point of view' (Cavell, 1979: 440). The notion of acknowledging humanity in others and in oneself is therefore a salient feature for enriching the proposed framework. Even though equal intelligence is at the core of equality, we contend that only when we begin to respect individuals as persons with dignity and as worthy citizens through their voices, can justice be enacted.

In Cavell's (1979) terms, caring for the other requires self-reflection of what you as the self might expect from the other, in this case the student's voice. This implies that both the carer and the cared-for need to reflect on their roles in such a relationship, and not necessarily to understand the reason for committing to the task. Underlining the role of committing to the pedagogical encounter shows an understanding of why caring ought to be expressed in this way, i.e. engaging in a provocative manner is not necessary, since both carer and cared-for may fail to understand each other at that point. Nevertheless, Cavell (1979) underscores acknowledging humanity in the self and the other as an approach that could drive, especially the caring educator's commitment towards a caring relationship. Firstly, if those (men) in AHE can see in women mirror images of themselves as humans (and not treat women as subordinate or inferior citizens), the possibility of patriarchal belief, male chauvinistic tendencies and power relationships could be eliminated – a process that would engender internal inclusion. Seeing the other as a human being demands that the dominant others – who possess all the power to control and dominate the Other (i.e. women) – depart from their authoritarian and inhuman practices of exclusion, and begin to treat the Other as an equal human being. To put it clearly, the assumption is that those with power (i.e. men in this context) may begin to demand internal inclusion for women by creating conditions to empower them, rather than women having to appeal continuously for inclusion. The argument we defend here is that treating certain human beings at face value and having them in HEIs without a voice is an injustice against humanity.

The point is that, by allowing some people to achieve formal access (physical representation) without giving them epistemological access – in Morrow (2007) terms referred to above – while subjecting them to internal exclusion and discrimination in AHE is an unjust act and cruelty to 'human possibility' (Cavell, 1979: 378). This caring relationship requires that men begin to establish ways to express their responsibility by including women and treating them as human beings, rather than as subordinates. In other words, men are expected to begin advocating for women's internal inclusion because the exclusion of the other becomes a challenge to their own humanity. Secondly, caring with respect underlies how the caring educator begins connecting to the Other (i.e. the cared-for student), which demands that one acknowledges humanity in the Other, and the basis for such action lies in oneself: 'I have to acknowledge humanity in the other, and the basis of it seems to lie in me' (Cavell, 1979: 433). In the same spirit, given that women's voices are internally excluded in higher education, demonstrates that there are uncaring relationships among people, especially when those in authority (mostly men) fail to acknowledge the humanity in them.

To care in the Cavell (1979) sense, ought to begin from the point of acknowledging others' inclusion and acting by challenging internal exclusion – an act that undermines humanity. In other words, the act of bringing women into HE deliberations and expecting them to assert their own voices is in itself a form of denying your own humanity and that of other. To exclude the other is to confirm that one (the dominant group) does not owe the other (internally excluded) respect as human beings. In such a situation, the failure of humanity with others reveals the failure of one's own humanity (Cavell, 1979: 434). People with authority to control internal engagement need to acknowledge themselves as humans and should consider others as humans who are equally worthy, as a matter of caring. In other words, respect for persons as a way of caring requires one with a voice to acknowledge the other as a person alongside him- or herself. The point is that we deny our responsibility if higher education continues to exclude women who will be deprived of their meaningful contributions as role models, mentors and other examples of good practices, such as connecting with 'the other', engaging with the differences of others and sharing their commonalities (Benhabib, 2002: 162). Cementing Benhabib's standpoint, Waghid (2008: 23) argues that democratic (AHE) institutions should nurture students and teachers with capabilities to take responsibility for their own ideas, to take intellectual risks, to develop a deep sense of respect for others, and to learn how to think critically with others in a democratic society. For this reason, considering African women's status and their inability to exercise their democratic rights through a voice, a paradigm shift transcending the gender divide is inevitable.

Summary: Re-imagining University Education – Towards Compassionate Responsibility

In defending a re-imagined university education, we argue that it is through deliberation that students could potentially disrupt the status quo and the taken-for-granted narrative and challenge the practices that impede a transformational agenda. Our contention is that we cannot expect people to care if they are not educated to do so. It is important to refer to what Assié-Lumumba (2006: 19) alluded to in relation to a university that is considered one of HEIs where men and women are educated with high levels of intellectual development in different fields. This pedagogical community is seen as vital where people are engaged in study and research. Only when a university takes its democratic responsibility of cultivating caring seriously, might internal exclusion and other forms of injustice be alleviated. Similarly, a university, as an integral social institution of a democratic society, should not only produce competitors in the world market, but also citizens who can strive for a just society. Nussbaum (2010) is concerned about treating education as if its main goal is to teach students to be economically productive, rather than to think critically and become knowledgeable and empathic citizens. To Nussbaum (2010: 6–7), nations, including those in Africa, and their social institutions must resist efforts to reduce education to a tool of gross national product, but should rather work towards education for a more inclusive type of citizenship that offers all students the capacity to be genuine democratic citizens of their countries and the world.

In sum, caring relationships should constitute three salient features: firstly, a caring relationship in university education needs compassionate imagining, where people listen to one another's lived experiences and put themselves in the shoes of other's misfortunes, and act to alleviate internal exclusion. Secondly, a caring relationship requires responsibility that enables the creation of conditions for people to exercise their equality of voice. This can happen when the dominant others (in this case, men) take responsibility to recognise humanity in themselves and the other by invoking their potentialities and being remorseful when others are internally excluded. Thirdly, a caring relationship calls for reasoning abilities that will enable people to become assertive and announce their presence as equal citizens. We contend that, if this reconstituted ethics of care is cultivated in higher education, Africa could have caring democratic citizens who will not only be deliberative, but who will also stand up against anomalies on the entire continent.

In essence, democratic AHE institutions, especially universities, ought to cultivate citizens, particularly women, with a voice, rather than using gender as a means for their inclusion. The salient take of this potential caring relationship recognises intellectual equality and is reciprocally caring, not for its own sake but for the sake of humanity. The point is that only when we begin to recognise all people as citizens of Africa and the world, might AHE caring relationships instil in citizens a sense of compassionate imagining and responsibility. In this way, individuals could exercise their citizenship through a voice as equally as possible in educational engagement, which could potentially engender substantive inclusion. In view of this, an apt way of caring offers a philosophically rich account that can both disrupt and possibly eliminate internal exclusion. Unless AHE institutions, especially universities, promote this potential caring relationship within their pedagogical encounters, it will be difficult, if not impossible, to cultivate caring citizens. Notably, this caring will not only help in attaining substantive inclusion, but may also engender social justice, which Africa and the entire world require.

References

Adetude, T. A., & Akensina, A. P. (2008). Factors affecting the standards of female education: A case study of senior secondary schools in the Kassena-Nankana District. *Journal of Social Sciences, 4*(4), 338–342.

Assié-Lumumba, N. (2006). *Higher education in Africa: Crises, reforms, and transformation.* Dakar, Senegal: Council for the Development of Social Science Research in Africa.

Assié-Lumumba, N. (Ed.). (2007). *Women and higher education in Africa: Reconceptualizing gender-based human capabilities and upgrading human rights to knowledge.* Abidjan, Côte d'Ivoire: CEPARRED.

Benhabib, S. (2002). *The claims of culture: Equality and diversity in the global era.* Princeton, NJ: Princeton University Press.

Butler, J. (1990). *Gender trouble: Feminism and the subversion of identity.* New York: Routledge.

Cavell, S. (1979). *The claim of reason: Wittgenstein, skepticism, morality and tragedy.* Oxford, UK: Clarendon.

Dunne, J., & Pendlebury, S. (2003). Practical reasoning. In N. Blake, P. Smeyers, R. Smith, & P. Standish (Eds.), *The Blackwell guide to the philosophy of education* (pp. 194–211). Oxford, UK: Blackwell.

Freire, P. (2004). *Pedagogy of hope: Reliving pedagogy of the oppressed.* New York: Continuum.

Gutmann, A., & Thompson, D. (2004). *Why deliberative democracy?* Princeton, NJ: Princeton University Press.

HERS-SA. (2008). *Institutional cultures and higher education: Where are the women?* A submission to the Stakeholder Summit on Higher Education Transformation, University of Cape Town. Retrieved August 23, 2011, from http://www.cepd.org.za/fuels/pictures/submission-stakeholders

Imam, A. (1997). Engendering African social sciences: An introductory essay. In A. Imam, A. Mama, & F. Sow (Eds.), *Engendering African social sciences* (pp. 1–30). Dakar, Senegal: CODESRIA.

Kiamba, J. (2008). Women and leadership positions: Social and cultural barriers to success. *Wagadu, 6,* 7–26.

King, E., & Mason, A. D. (2001). *Engendering development through gender equality in rights, resources and voice.* Washington, DC: The World Bank/Oxford University Press.

Kwesiga, J. C. (2002). *Women's access to higher education in Africa: Uganda's experience.* Kampala, Uganda: Fountain.

Leathwood, C., & Read, B. (2009). *Gender and the changing face of higher education: A feminized future.* New York: Open University Press.

London Institute of Education. (2005). *Gender equity in Commonwealth Higher Education.* Working articles 1–5. Retrieved August 22, 2011, from http://www.ioewebserver.ioe.ac.uk/ioe/cms/get.asp?cid

Maürtin-Cairncross, A. (2013). A still-chilly climate: Experiences of women in leadership positions in South African higher education. *Global Perspective, Association of American Colleges and Universities, 38*(1). Retrieved September 19, 2013, from http://www.aacu.org/ocww/volume38_1/global.cfm?printer_friendly=1

Morley, L. (2004). *Gender and access in Commonwealth higher education.* Paper presented at the First Colloquium on Research and Higher Education Policy, Paris.

Morley, L. (2012). Widening participation in Ghana and Tanzania. *International Journal of Higher Education, 67*, 21–23.

Morrow, W. (2007). *Learning to teach in South Africa*. Cape Town, South Africa: HSRC Press.

NEPAD (New Partnership for Africa's Development). (2002). *Foreign and Commonwealth Office*. Retrieved July 16, 2011, from http://www.nepad.org/

Noddings, N. (1984). *Caring: A feminine approach to ethics and moral education*. Berkeley, CA: University of California Press.

Noddings, N. (1992). *The challenge to care in schools: An alternative approach to education*. New York: Teachers College Press.

Nussbaum, M. C. (2001). *Upheavals of thought: The intelligence of emotions*. Cambridge, UK: Cambridge University Press.

Nussbaum, M. C. (2010). *Not for profit: Why democracy needs the humanities*. Princeton, NJ: Princeton University Press.

Obi, C. (2003). *Emergent female power in popular struggles in Nigeria: Women movements in the Niger Delta*. Paper present at the International Workshop on Emergent Economy, Institute of Developing Economy, Tokyo, Japan.

Onokala, P. C., & Onah, F. O. (1998). *Women in academic positions in the universities in Nigeria*. Research report prepared for the Association of African Universities – A Special Project Under the Study Programme on Higher Education Management in Africa.

Rancière, J. (1992). *The ignorant schoolmaster: Five lessons in intellectual emancipation* (K. Ross, Trans.). Stanford, CA: Stanford University Press.

Rancière, J. (1999). *Disagreement: Politics and philosophy*. London: Minnesota University Press.

Shanyanana, R. N. (2011). *Education for democratic citizenship and cosmopolitanism: The case of the Republic of Namibia*. Unpublished Master's Thesis, Stellenbosch University, Stellenbosch, South Africa.

Slote, M. (2007). *The ethics of care and empathy*. New York/London, UK: Routledge.

Tamale, S. (Ed.). (2011). *African sexualities: A reader*. Cape Town, South Africa: Pambazuka Press.

Teferra, D., & Altbach, P. (2004). African higher education: Challenges for the 21st century. *Higher Education, 47*(1), 221–250.

UNESCO (United Nations Educational, Scientific and Cultural Organization). (1998). *Gender and higher education – A sea change*. Report on the thematic debate entitled Women in higher education: Issues and perspectives. World Conference on Higher Education, Paris. Retrieved March 3, 2013, from http://www.uis.unesco.org/Education/Pages/women-higher-education.aspx

UNESCO UIS (United Nations Educational, Scientific and Cultural Organization Institute for Statistics). (2010). *Comparing education statistics across the world: Special focus on gender.* Global Education Digest. Retrieved March 15, 2013, from http://www.uis.unesco.org/Library/Documents/GED_2010_EN.pdf

United Nations MDGs (Millennium Development Goals). (2005). *Taking action: Achieving gender equality and empowering women.* Report prepared by the Taskforce on Education and Gender. New York: UN Millennium Project.

Waghid, Y. (2008). Democratic citizenship, education and friendship revisited: In defence of democratic justice. *Studies in Philosophy of Education, 27*, 197–206.

Wagner-Martin, L. (1994). *Telling women's lives: The new biography.* New Brunswick, NJ: Rutgers University Press.

Young, I. M. (2000). *Inclusion and democracy.* Princeton, NJ: Princeton University Press.

14

Coda: Educational Technology, Pedagogy and Caring

Introduction

Much of the online pedagogical work we have been doing with staff and students at the university where we work, connects with Yusef Waghid's articulation of rhythmic caring within dissonant pedagogical encounters. We find his notion of rhythmic caring quite provocative and relevant to the work we have been doing with staff and students at a university of technology. Like Waghid, we too are attracted to the notion of rhythmic caring where we give and take and hold back and release our articulations within our pedagogical encounters. In the first instance, dissonant pedagogical encounters take into account the possibility that discomfort, practical criticism, and scepticism would underscore our online interactions with staff and students. Secondly, as we show in this chapter, our implementation of Waghid's idea of rhythmic caring within dissonant pedagogical encounters is a way by which we can make our work with educational technology and pedagogy more provocative, risky and transformative.

By Faiq Waghid and Zayd Waghid – Cape Peninsula University of Technology

Faiq's Explication of Care Through Educational Technology

As an undergraduate student, I recall leaving many a lecture, frustrated by the dominant 'chalk and talk' teacher-centred approach to pedagogy adopted by some university teachers. This sentiment was often shared by my peers attending lectures with me, as we yearned to engage more constructively with our teachers. Through this frustration and a general interest in innovative technologies, I consequently decided to pursue a career in education, drawing on my interest in Information and Communication Technologies (ICT), to explore how my own educational practices could be enhanced. As a young educator, I felt accountable to provide my students more than what they were traditionally accustomed to from older generations of teachers. This ultimately led to the realisation of a PhD in Curriculum Studies, more specifically on how social networking sites as educational technologies, could support a wide range of teaching and learning expectations.

Nowadays I work as an educational technologist at the Cape Peninsula University of Technology (CPUT). One of my core responsibilities is to assist academics to explore the role educational technologies can play as part of their pedagogical initiation. In general, my consultations begin with a basic interest displayed by a lecturer on using a particular tool. As there is a plethora of educational technologies with a wide range of affordances, ensuring lecturers match the affordances of a specific tool with the teaching and learning need is of paramount importance to pedagogy.

In a deliberative sphere, characterised by criticism, we explore how their proposed use of technology addresses a specific teaching and learning requirement, rather than using technology for the sake of using it. Many of these discussions are inherently characterised by moments of discomfort, as academics realise that they are not prioritising a teaching and learning need, but are, instead, trying to use technology as an add-on or gimmick. Additionally, our discussions are characterised by moments of practical criticism, as academics share their unique educational contexts and rationale for why they feel a specific implementation of an educational technology would be most effective. Through critical feedback, these lecturers are able to devise more justifiable elucidations of how educational technologies could augment teaching and learning. Through these consultations, characterised by momentary instances of dissonant action, feedback and consequent justifications, our to-and-fro oscillations of rupturing and caring – that is, rhythmic caring, we are able to devise more meaningful learning experiences for students collectively.

Educational technologies may allow us to support the needs of an inherently heterogeneous student cohort. For instance, students learn at different paces. Some students are able to comprehend concepts covered in curricula faster than others. Podcasting lectures is seen as a viable educational technology, as students' understandings may be reinforced by them (i.e. the students) listening to recordings of their lecturers. Furthermore, educational technologies, such as podcasts, are also able to support the special learning needs of some students. Another prevalent means of podcasting that can be seen as an illustration of how educational technologies is used in rhythmic caring, particularly in HE contexts, is through the adoption of what is commonly referred to as the flipped classroom. A flipped classroom, also dubbed flipped-based approaches to pedagogy or flipped pedagogies, encourages lecturers to use teaching time more meaningfully and attentively, by putting emphasis on student engagement in the classroom, rather than focusing on the dissemination of only content. In this way, it is envisaged that content dissemination could occur via the medium of a podcast to which a student could listen prior to the classroom encounter. In fostering rhythmic caring, these podcasts should be of a conceptual nature. Concepts covered in podcasts can then be re-enacted through classroom deliberations. As students share their conceptual understanding, there exist opportunities for rupturing and nurturing through rigorous feedback provided by lecturers. In terms of this to-and-fro oscillation of rupturing and caring, i.e. rhythmic caring, there always exists an opportunity for the realisation of more justifiable understandings of concepts and practices on the part of university teachers and students engaged in deliberative pedagogical encounters.

Another well-known integration of educational technology with which I am currently engaged in order to augment teaching and learning, is that of learning management systems (LMSs). LMSs are typically used for the administration, tracking and delivery of educational experiences for students. Lecturer to student ratios are typically high. Having an LMS that could administer and track the needs of a sizeable and similarly diverse student cohort, retrospectively and in some instances pre-emptively, could be seen as invaluable for teaching and learning. For instance, students who are not performing in their online academic activities, such as submitting assignments, or students who are performing poorly in online formative tests, can be flagged automatically by an LMS. Interventions can then be arranged with the students flagged; thus, affording lecturers the opportunity to provoke students into a moment of discomfort. Through these instances of dissonant action, there exist opportunities for practical criticism and scepticism. Students can engage critically with the work introduced by teachers and in turn, they (i.e. the students) can begin to question the point of their learning.

In a deliberative space, lecturers can provide rigorous feedback, encouraging students towards better understandings of concepts and practices. An LMS can consequently be seen as a tool to foster opportunities for rhythmic caring. Another example, of how LMSs offer opportunities for the initiation of rhythmic caring, can be seen in the extensive use of assessments for learning, in particular formative assessments. Assessments such as these, in the form of online quizzes, are based on objective-type questions, including true or false, multiple choice and, column matching question types. These objective question types can be used in automated assessments. Lecturers can set up feedback prompts based on a students' selection. For instance, if a student incorrectly responds to a multiple-choice question, the LMS can be set up to provide a student automatically with remedial feedback based on the wrong selection. Feedback may serve as an impetus for rigorous critical assessment of both the pedagogical enactments of lecturers and students, and in turn, the possibility of rhythmic caring manifesting would become highly likely.

Educational technologies have also played important roles in negating logistical constraints for students. For instance, students are not all afforded the opportunity to stay close to the universities where they are enrolled, resulting in demanding travelling schedules. These constraints may be exacerbated when students are required to submit group work assignments. Coordinating dates and times at a time after lectures, and engaging in group work favour mostly students staying close to campus. Here the Google Collaborative suite, as an educational technology, comprising applications such as Docs and Slides, afford students the opportunity to participate in group writing or group presentations free from temporal or spatial constraints, provided they have Internet connectivity. Students are able to work on a single slide show or to write simultaneously, without having to email one another's individual contributions for subsequent collation. What distinguishes this educational technology from traditional word processing applications is that is allows for real-time collaborative writing. Students work on a single piece of work and are aided by built-in chat features, video conferencing tools, and tracking changes that update in real time. Lecturers are able to initiate students in encounters with the support of the latter affordances. What follows are opportunities for this educational technology to serve as a platform facilitating the to-and-fro oscillations of rupturing and caring, towards students building more meaningful arguments or justifications comprising their work.

Educational technologies are also being used to further student writing skills. Although primarily used for the detection of similarity with other pieces of work, software such as Turnitin and Safeassign, are performing valuable roles, such as supplementing students' transition from high school to university. For many students developing referencing and citation skills, on which they will rely throughout their student lives, can be a daunting task. The arduous task of having to facilitate the development of these skills falls on lecturers. Lecturers are expected to scrutinise students' reference lists, citations or whether they have simply copied and pasted items from the Internet every time they submit a piece of writing. This situation seems quite impractical to say the least. Additionally, students require prompt feedback on their work, ensuring that their emerging writing skills are consolidated and advanced.

Educational technologies such as Turnitin and Safeassign are able to support students in a multitude of ways. These tools can generate similarity reports, highlighting to students whether they are using citations and references incorrectly. These reports colour code each reference and the corresponding citation, thus providing an easy-to-interpret report. My experience in higher education has seen similarity reports resulting in tremendous discomfort, as students, and sometimes academics, vehemently deny plagiarising pieces of work. Despite similarity reports not being an exact indication of plagiarism at times, many students incorrectly interpret these reports to be of a plagiarised nature. What follows are encounters of dissonant action, where students engage in rigorous feedback, providing justifications for their pieces of work. Invariably, these engagements facilitate the development of students' writing skills. These engagements can be seen as instances where rhythmic caring is enacted, because such engagements are stimulated by provocation, reflexivity and openness. The similarity detection software, like the other educational technologies discussed earlier, shows how educational technologies facilitate rhythmic caring, as students and academics are provided reports of their similarity indexes. In addition, in the event that a similarity index is high, such students and academics are required to comply with a minimum similarity index in the sense that they are now obliged to reduce the similarity. In turn, university lecturers evaluate the revised pieces of writing and make judgements that are provided to students and other academics in terms of the newly reconstructed pieces of writing.

Zayd's Elucidation of Care Through Online Encounters

When I embarked on a journey towards higher education having completed a doctoral study in the field of education together with the experience that I acquired when teaching at a historically disadvantaged school for more than six years, I had certain expectations of teaching at an HEI. One such expectation of a university educator – at least from my own experiences of formal tertiary studies as a student in South Africa – is that a university student (other than a school learner) is one who is expected to engage actively and critically with his or her lecturers and peers. As a former high school teacher, my experiences of teaching school learners were that learners expect to be taught along the principles of rote learning. Rote learning is a practice that continues to permeate many South African schools as a result of a stringent curriculum policy statement despite the intended outcomes of the policy aimed at fostering critical thinking among school learners. Notwithstanding the apparent and intended outcomes of the school curriculum in South Africa, the teacher continues to provide information with the learner unassumingly regurgitating this information and subsequently being assessed in some formal examination.

As a teacher, there are a number of roles that one should simultaneously and collaboratively enact. And, by collaborating with others I refer specifically to the pedagogical relationship a teacher develops with his or her students. As a teacher, one may identify yourself as a leader, mediator, curriculum initiator, researcher, pastor, mentor, assessor and subject specialist. I do not mean to say that these roles ought to change in the HE environment, but rather, such roles ought to transform the pedagogical competencies of the teacher in line with the type of learner taught in an HE environment. My expectation of teaching in higher education was that a university student takes a rather active role in his or her own learning while the university educator plays a facilitative role. The university educator poses higher-order cognitive questions in traditional classroom settings, and is concomitantly treated with equally intellectual responses provided by students. Thus, the transition from a secondary school teacher to a university educator, by implication, means that the latter would be more accommodating – at least in South Africa, as a result of exercising greater autonomy in the higher academe – to an engaging and deliberative environment premised on active and critical learning.

Considering that I left a school in which the implementation of educational technology was still in its infancy stage, my expectations of teaching in higher education and more specifically the students whom I would be teaching were premised on the notion that the students themselves would be digitally literate and capable university students taking into account the era around technology in schools in South Africa. In this regard, I found myself quite privileged to be teaching in an HE environment. In view of the fact that many of the students whom I was now teaching emanated from historically disadvantaged backgrounds, I soon realised that there were inherent challenges that were evident but initially invisible to me as a result of my high expectations of teaching university students. In fact, it was instances of students not being accustomed to technology commensurate with their demonstrated fear towards using these technologies that heightened my consciousness towards (re)examining my own identity as a university educator in relation to the culture of my students having emanated from schools where rote learning is so routinely practiced.

Being confronted with university students stemming from a school environment where the traditional 'chalk and talk' style is very much prevalent, especially in many historically disadvantaged South African schools, was quite a daunting task, particularly when the intended outcome of the HE lesson was aimed at fostering meaningful debates and discussions. For one, such university students are accustomed to functioning in isolated silos in lecture rooms expecting of a university educator to convey information as a practice of routine thinking and learning. For a university educator to talk and to give, one would expect a student in turn, to give back. When this form of interaction did not transpire in my own lectures with my students, it subsequently required of me to scrutinise my own pedagogical practices and identity as a university educator. Not being able to use educational technology efficaciously further exacerbates the level of learning, especially when a university teacher has certain expectations of students and students concomitantly have expectations of the type of learning needed to progress.

Amartya Sen (2007) provides an important account of making sense of one's identity. For Sen (2007) one's affiliation to a particular group can be quite important, depending on the particular context. However, for Sen (2007: 19), the recognition of identities is robustly plural in that the importance of one's identity not necessarily needs to obliterate the importance of other identities. By implication, for my own teaching, this meant that my identity as a pastor would not take preference over my role as an advocate for critical learning in my classes. Rather my identity as a pastor and advocate for critical learning would be premised on Waghid's explication of showing rhythmic caring towards my students. This meant that I had to situate myself in the context of my students coming from a school system where their voices are seemingly silenced in many autocratic classrooms in South Africa.

As a former student myself, I often appreciated an intellectual discussion in class regarding a contentious topic. Situating myself in the contexts of my students played an important role in reflecting critically on my own position as a university educator and a former undergraduate student. I was now required to imagine myself as a student who, during lessons, may feel anxious when responding to a university educator in class. Such a student, expecting a response to a question with which he or she is confronted, but perhaps lacking adequate knowledge to respond eloquently, is drawn into an act of deliberation. In order to create a platform where my students' voices would be more forthcoming required of me to explore how the use of educational technology, which Faiq Waghid explained in the previous section, could create spaces necessary for my students, who are often silenced in school contexts, to deliberate and engage equitably with university teachers.

The rationale behind using online engagements in my own teaching soon developed and became premised on the notion that by cultivating a community of inquiry, the students and I would be exposed to situations where our social, cognitive and teaching competencies in the online engagements would be enhanced (Garrison, Anderson, & Archer, 2001). The latter claim is based on an understanding that face-to-face contexts would benefit from effective online engagements (Waghid, 2016). I cannot recall ever unjustifiably dismissing a student who experienced using technology quite challenging or daunting in my own teaching and learning. Neither have I ridiculed students for not responding to my questions posed in classes. Usually, as a university educator, my correspondence to my students would be to create pedagogical spaces in which they are afforded the means to ask questions while I as university educator would invariably respond to their concerns without diminishing the use of technology in class. Thus, without excluding students who lacked the technological competencies and who were not able to perform their roles as students efficaciously in their own learning, learning in my classes became much more attuned to online deliberative engagements.

Having initiated a blended learning approach in my own teaching in which I use my current institution's LMS concurrently with face-to-face classes, served as a means to expose my students to online pedagogical approaches in the schools where they would perhaps one day teach. Recently, in the Western Cape Provincial Government's education department has started introducing its After School Game Changer programme which, includes ensuring access to ICT at schools in the Western Cape region. By implication, this would render more effective and active learning in schools, which would require adept and competent teachers serving the profession. Hence, the rationale for my own teaching is corroborated by the need to prepare my students for changing and dynamic school contexts.

To my mind, I have been extremely accommodating to my students' needs while maintaining an environment premised on cultivating the competencies of my students as digitally literate pre-service teachers. The support that I give my students in their online engagements is underscored by discomfort, practical criticism and scepticism. I refer to discomfort in the sense that the probing questions that I offer to my students in our online engagements require of them to start reflecting on the (un)known by transforming themselves into distinct contexts without creating an environment of uncertainty. In fact, it was the sense of discomfort that was required of them to break away from the isolated silos, which were prevalent in the majority of my classes. However, engaging with my students in online contexts does not consequentially mean that I accept all their arguments at face value. In this regard, I am critical of their opinions in a deliberative manner, taking into account their points of view but not unjustifiably dismissing their points of view. Although I am sceptical of their comments and offer practical criticisms of their views I am nonetheless attuned to Yusef Waghid's exercise of rhythmic caring in the ensuing approval of my students' points of view on the online platforms available to them.

I consider my online engagement with my students as a responsibility towards cultivating socially conscious teachers along the principles of social justice in an African context. What I want my students to develop, is for them to make sense of their pedagogical encounters with their peers and myself in the production of their arguments. In the engagements with my students, issues of social injustice, such as poverty, inequality and social deprivation are among the many contentious themes in my classes, which are discussed as a means of cultivating in them the desire to demonstrate care for others as part of a community. We all belong to distinct groups; however, it is an acknowledgement that a community is an extension of one's identity that is tantamount to claiming that one's success is dependent on the community and vice versa (Sen, 2007: 5). In other words, I wanted to inculcate in my students a sense of *ubuntu* as a means of breaking away from the isolated silos while showing care for the other. As Sen (2007: 25) avers:

Coda: Educational Technology, Pedagogy and Caring 169

Our ability to think clearly may, of course, vary with training and talent, but we can, as adult and competent human beings, question and begin to challenge what has been taught to us if we are given the opportunity to do so.

While I was sceptical and critical of my students' arguments, it was not difficult for them to realise my pursuit towards creating an environment premised on discomfort in developing opportunities for them to enhance their academic capacities as university students.

I hold that online pedagogical spaces are necessary for inculcating in university students an inclination to take risks in their encounters. By taking risks I do not imply that they ought to become dismissive of their peers or my points of view. Rather, I suggest that they become appreciative of our intellectual pedagogical encounters. In fact, taking risks in online encounters creates the possibility for university students to come up with (un)imaginable solutions to the most pressing concerns permeating society through contentious debates and discussions. And, when students learn to take risks, they learn to produce plausible arguments without an aversion to being corrected by me or their peers. By implication, they take risks without the possibility of being chastised or told that their responses are perhaps illogical or incomprehensible. They are also not afraid to modify their points of view when they are self-reflecting critically on their own arguments.

I have argued thus far that students' online engagements should always be treated with rhythmic caring. When students' comments are considered as disjointed and uncorroborated statements, then (HE) educators should caringly point this out to university students, particularly students who are not deemed by the lecturers as digitally literate. Of course, not all students are capable of producing plausible arguments and points of view on online platforms, but if students have made rigorous efforts to reflect on their comments and reproduce justifiable arguments, educators should display appreciation of their students' work. I consider myself an HE educator who takes into account students' arguments with care, and I have shown that I am far more interested in enhancing the fluidity of my students work than just submitting to the demand of creating an online presence or having some gimmick, as Faiq Waghid previously mentioned. By this I mean, that as an HE educator, I would consider informing students whose comments are not meticulously sound, with kindness and those students with valid points of view, with appreciation. Like Yusef Waghid, I do not hold the view that unsympathetic and dismissive comments should ever be sent to university students. However, I equally do not disagree with a practice of informing my students whether their work lacks substance. My caring is, therefore, enacted in relation to pointing out limitations in my students' work. In this way, the care that I bring to online encounters could be considered as in tune with rhythm.

In this chapter, we have shown that, through online pedagogical encounters, rhythmic caring reveals itself in encounters with us as university educators and students respectively. Such pedagogical encounters, as Yusef Waghid has advocated for throughout this book, are expressive of our views on pedagogical encounters and constituted by discomfort, practical criticism and scepticism. Firstly, university students experience a sense of discomfort when they are told that their responses require more meaningful thought and reflection. Secondly, our collective encounters are instigated by moments of practical criticism. Students realise that their comments are not taken at face value and they are, therefore, evaluated and assessed on their points of view in a deliberative manner. In response to the critical feedback, they respond and critically reflect equally on their points of view with more justifiable arguments. Thirdly, in reviewing their comments, we adopt an approach of suspicion as we challenge them to make their statements more articulate and consistent. Through to-and-fro instances of rhythmic caring, the opportunity exists for university students to construct and reconstruct more defensible online comments. In other words, students are provoked to become more critical and insightful in our online encounters to produce more credible pedagogical engagements. In this way, our pedagogical encounters are deemed to be provocative, risky and transformative.

Summary

In this chapter, we have offered a reflective account of our caring relationships with academics and university students. In both occurrences, our pedagogical encounters are informed by an ethic of care that resonates with discomfort, scepticism and practical criticism. Inasmuch as our encounters are premised on rhythmic caring, we do not remain unaware that the recipients of care, that is, our colleagues and students, also confirm our encounter with them as one of provocation, risk-taking and transformation.

References

Garrison, D. R., Anderson, T., & Archer, W. (2001). Critical thinking, cognitive presence, and computer conferencing in distance education. *American Journal of Distance Education, 15*(1), 7–23.

Sen, A. (2007). *Identity and violence: The illusion of destiny*. London: Penguin Books.

Waghid, Z. (2016). Using film and online group blogs to cultivate a community of inquiry: A case studied at a university of technology in South Africa. *Progressio, 38*(2), 106–131.

Index

A

Academic, v, 39, 59, 68, 98, 103–108, 110, 111, 160, 163, 170
  capacities, 169
  inquiry, xviii, 110, 111
  journals, 98
  pursuits, 103, 106, 110, 111
  university, 107–109

Access
  epistemological, 136, 137, 152
  formal, 136, 152
  notion of, 136

Act
  admirable, 21
  affirming, 20
  afraid to, 139
  attention, 50
  authentically, xvi, 26, 78
  authority, 26
  autonomy, 26, 28, 29
  care, 22, 110, 115, 150
  community, 21, 22
  compassion, 124
  confirmation, 20
  freely, 29, 61
  hostility, 9
  humanity, 28
  inclusion, 2–8, 11
  justice, 82
  relationality, 6, 8, 14 (*see also* Relational act)
  respectful, 21
  responsibility, 11
  in a therapeutic manner, 28

Action
  dialogical, 17, 22
  human, 1, 127
  just, 66, 149
  pedagogical, 33, 60, 105
  practical, 13
  responsible, 9

Index

Active attention, 49, 50
Africa, xvi, xviii, xx, 4, 32, 55, 59, 82, 85, 90, 93, 95, 98, 101, 107, 113, 114, 117–121, 126, 127, 131–134, 136, 144, 147, 154, 155
  higher education in, 137
  liberation in, 130
  universities in, 135, 142
African
  communities, 94, 108, 117
  continent, xix, 31, 35, 68, 89, 93, 94, 99–101, 105–109, 118, 127, 129
  countries, 82, 123, 130, 131, 134, 141
  democratic citizenship education, 82
  philosophy of education, 4
  scholars, 35, 99, 119, 143
  societies, 94, 107, 108, 149
  students, 89
  teaching, 89
  teaching and learning, 90
  universities, xix, 90, 93–95, 98, 99, 109, 116, 134, 135
  women, 146, 153
Anger, xv, 25, 45, 51
Apartheid
  police, 26, 27, 29
  years, 4, 30
Arguments, x–xii, 14, 15, 17, 21, 27, 76, 98, 101, 102, 139, 163, 168, 170
  construct, 15, 17
  deconstruct, 15, 17
  discourse of, 15
  justifiable, 169
  plausible, 65, 169
  rational, 118
  reconstruct, 15, 17
  rigour of, 14, 15
  students, 169
Attachment, vi, xii, xvii, 4, 9, 25, 27, 71, 78, 115
  human (*see* Human, attachment)
Attentive/attention, xii, xiii, xvii, 5, 17, 50–52, 55, 61, 71, 83, 84, 87, 110, 114, 125, 147
  active (*see* Active attention)
  care, 52, 53, 117
  listening, 147
Attentiveness, xvii, xx, 28, 43, 46, 51, 55, 71, 84, 92
Authenticity, v, xiii, xvi, 2, 22, 27, 28, 30–36, 39, 42, 61, 64, 71, 130
  un-authenticity, 71
Authors, 29, 98–100, 102, 110, 111
Autonomy, xv, 26, 28, 29, 31, 65, 66, 85, 94, 127, 165
  individual, 32

Behaviour
  aggressive, 7
  belligerent, 7
  distressful, 7
  neuro-psychological, vi
  of the student, 65
  violent, 91
Beliefs
  moral, 7
Black
  academics, 4, 99
  scholars, 99
  scholarship (*see* Scholarship, black)

Index

C

Care/caring, v–vii, ix–xvi, xx, 1, 3–6, 8, 11, 13–22, 27–29, 32, 33, 40, 49, 50, 53, 56, 58, 60, 61, 64, 72–75, 79, 81, 83, 89, 94, 100, 104, 106, 109, 110, 115, 117, 124, 126, 149, 150, 153, 154, 161, 163
  act, 8, 21, 109, 123
  approach, 148
  aspects of, 26, 97
  attentive, xvii, 49, 50, 52–54, 77
  authentic, xvi, 22, 30–36, 43
  cared-for, 13, 15, 18, 28, 43, 50, 79, 99, 115, 148–153
  conception of, 148
  cosmopolitan, xviii, 80, 81, 83–87, 97
  democratic, xvii, 55–61, 63, 97
  detachment from, 71
  dialogical relation, 18
  dimensions of, xviii, 90, 97
  dyadic, 55, 58, 60–61
  educative practices, 108
  educator, 151
  empathic, xvii, xviii, 63, 65–69, 76, 83, 87
  ethical, 9, 29
  ethicist, 55
  Freirean pedagogy, 33
  -givers, 46, 48, 50, 64, 74
  -giving, 46, 49
  ideas on, xvi, 26
  inclusive, xvi, 4, 5, 11, 13, 43
  individuals, 141
  instance of, 15
  interaction, 49, 50
  manifestation, xvi, 2, 6, 15, 69
  moral aspect, 46
  notions of, xii, xvii–xix, 20, 27, 39, 40, 43, 61, 63, 64, 72, 80, 83, 97
  openness to, 27
  for the other, 152
  with others, vi, xvii, 56, 61, 116
  pedagogy of, xiv, 27
  practical, 43
  pragmatic, xvi, 36, 41–43, 45, 47, 48
  public institution, 141
  quality of, 50
  receivers, 46, 48, 50
  receiving, 46, 49
  recipients of, 110, 171
  relations, xviii, 14, 17, 110
  relationships of, 17, 18, 39, 60, 84, 87, 110, 145, 149, 150, 152, 154, 155, 170
  responsibilities for, 56
  rhythmic, vi, xi, xiv, xv, xvii–xix, 71, 72, 74–81, 86, 87, 89, 92, 97, 99, 102, 103, 105–110, 159, 161, 162, 164, 166, 168–171
  socializing, 43
  for the soul, 51
  for students, xii, 5, 10, 26–30, 32, 44
  of a teacher, 76
  transactional, xvii, 36, 40, 41, 43–45, 47, 48, 50
  ubuntu, xviii, 90–95, 97
  uncaring, 40
  uncaring relationships, 153
  virtue of, 2

Index

Carers, xiii, xvi, 13–15, 110, 148–150, 152
  authentic, 64
  cosmopolitan, 85, 86
  pragmatic, 44
Change, xiii, xvi, xviii, 20, 22, 30, 35, 51, 58, 59, 68, 85, 86, 91, 105, 107, 108, 116, 118–121, 139, 146, 165
  meaningful, 126
  political, 32
  practical, 20
  social, 32, 33, 140
Citizens
  informed, 94
  responsible, 130
  worthy, 152
Citizenship, 8, 31, 55, 82, 93, 101, 125, 155
  education
    democratic, xix, 31, 32, 55, 93, 94, 101
  inclusive, 154
Classroom, 79, 161
  autocratic, 166
  deliberations, 161
  encounter, 161
  flipped, 161
  settings, 165
Colonial, 93, 94, 105, 120
  authorities, 93
  rule, 93
  Western, 130
Colonialism, 93, 106, 122, 130
Colour, 132
  people of, 40
Commonalities, 83, 153
Communication, 6, 9, 115
  channels of, 139
  democratic, 9
  kinds of, 117
  political, 10
  process of, 133
Community, v, ix, x, xx, 3, 21, 34, 35, 41, 43, 45, 47, 67, 85, 102, 108, 133, 134, 147, 150, 154, 167, 168
  defence of, x
  deliberative, xi
  democratic, x
  intersubjective, ix
Compassion, xv, xviii, 26, 63, 90, 91, 120, 121, 124, 125, 148–151
  act of, 121–126
  embodying, 123
  emotion of, 150
  unconditional, 125–127
Compassionate, xix, 92, 122, 123, 130, 149, 150
  imagining, 149–151, 154, 155
  responsibility, 154–155
Concept of care, x, 113
Confirmation, 14–22
  act of, 20
  notion of, 20
Conflict, xv, 14, 29, 44, 109, 126
Connection, 7, 8, 64, 108
  internal, 33
  relational, 3
  relationship of (*see* Relationship, of connection)
Consciousness, 165

critical, 30
of freedom, 32
state of, 13
Construct, xiii, 14, 21, 45, 101, 143, 170
social, 143
Content, 115
delivery, 113
dissemination, 161
Conversation, xx, 17, 92, 118
disrupt, 147
Cosmopolitanism, xviii, 44, 81, 83, 84, 87
Courage, 11, 21, 45
Credibility, 27, 99
of authors, 99
intellectual, 104
of scholarly work, 100
Critical
consciousness, 30
judgement, 45
reflection, xix, 66, 78, 95
thinking, 145, 164
thinking skills, 145
voices, 30
Criticality, 34, 94, 99, 116–118, 126
Critically reflective, 28, 30, 36
Criticism, xiv, xviii, 3, 9, 15, 32, 34, 113, 160
practical, 102, 159, 160, 162, 168, 170
Cultural
agency, 116–118, 126
background, 131
claims, 117
concerns, 94

differences, 10, 68, 90
dominance, 127
engagement, 117
identity, 118
imperialism, 67
justifications, 117
labour, 118
markers, 85
persuasion, 120
position, 2
practices, 129
privileges, 122
understanding, 67
ways of seeing the world, 118
Culture of exclusion, 45

D

Debate, v–vii, 17, 18, 110, 132
moderate, 113
Decision-making, 9, 14, 133–135, 138, 142
Decolonised/decoloniality, 59, 93–95, 99, 105–110, 119–121, 123, 125, 127
African university, 93
notion of, 120
practice of, 106
role, 94
Deconstruct, 15, 17, 101
Deliberation, 5, 8, 9, 17, 36, 91, 94, 109, 117, 126, 127, 133, 141, 149, 153, 154, 167
classroom, 161
democratic, 149
public, 134

Democracy, ix, xv, xx, 26, 32, 71, 132, 143
  action, 9, 17
  agenda, 4
  citizens, 56, 154, 155
  conversation, 57
  deliberation, 149
  education, xxi, 17, 33–36, 40, 45, 52, 63
  education curriculum, 34
  engagement, 33, 61, 110
  environment, 132
  idea of, 55
  inclusion, 8–10
  justice, 58
  participation, 34
  politics, 56
  processes, 133, 142, 151
  responsibility, 154
  social, 36
  society, 56, 130–134, 153, 154
  values of, 93
  virtues, 132
Democratisation, 5, 33
Demographic profile, 103, 107
Detachment, vi, xii, xvii, 4, 71, 78, 113
Dialogue, xvii, 14–22, 30, 32
  form of, 17
  open-endedness, 18
  participants in, 17
Differences, 2, 6, 7, 67, 83, 92, 115, 133, 148, 153
  biological, 143
  cultural, 90
  ethnic, 90
  political, 90
  religious, 68
Dignity, xvii, 28, 63, 67, 69, 89, 91, 109, 114, 115, 151
  sense of, 95
Disadvantaged, vi, 30, 58, 107, 165
  backgrounds, 149
  communities, 115
  economically, 115
  groups, 140, 141
  historically, 137, 164, 166
  previously, 123
Discernment, 51, 53
Discourse, 5, 99, 118, 140
  of African philosophy of education, 85
  of argumentation, 15
  of articulation, 34
  constructed, 143
  of deliberative inquiry, 116
  democratic, 133
  educational, 147
  HE, 110, 122, 123
  of learning, 15
  of moral education, 14
  public, 134
  theoretical, 117
  of un-criticality, 34
Discrimination, 29, 35, 137, 152
Discussion, 17, 30, 45, 58, 61, 66, 68, 72, 74, 85, 93, 118, 119, 134, 138
  intellectual, 166
  point, 106–107
Disrespect, 5, 65, 90
Dissensus, 6, 9, 18–20, 58
Dissonance, vi, xix, 44, 103
  atmosphere of, xiv
Diversity, 45, 103, 104, 107
Dyadic, 55, 58, 60–61
  model, 60
  relationship, 60

Index

Economic
  advancement, 117
  class, 115
  development, 131
  disadvantaged, 115
  insecurity, 86
  productive, 154
  shocks, 84
  underdevelopment, 116
  welfare, 137
Education
  in Africa, 5
  deliberations, 145, 146
  deliberative democratic, 34–36
  democratic (*see* Democracy, education)
  development, 59, 61
  engagement, 155
  hegemonic, 119
  higher (*see* Higher education)
  implications, 32, 86
  institutions, xviii, 31, 95, 131
  interests, 27
  as liberation, 27
  moral, 17
  as a pedagogy of caring, 27
  practices, 160
  system, 132
  technologies, 160–164
  theories, ix, xi, xix, 72, 101
  universal primary, 130, 136
  university, xiii, 90, 123, 129, 131–142, 147, 154–155
Educator, 26, 64, 145, 147–149, 151, 166, 169
  carer, 150
  caring, 152, 153
  HE, 169
  university, 164–167, 170
  young, 160
Emancipation, 19, 20, 33
  of the self, 20
Emotion, xv, 74, 111, 138, 149, 150
  of compassion, 150
  complex, 51
  distracting, 7
  human, 74
  impetus, 149
  intelligence, 138
  judgement, 150
  significant, 149
Empathy, xv, xvii, 28, 63–69, 71, 76, 81, 83, 87, 114
  citizens, 154
Encounters, xii, xx, 2, 4, 5, 10, 11, 20, 27, 28, 35, 44, 45, 47, 51, 52, 58, 60, 64–66, 71, 74, 76–80, 85, 87, 89, 91, 92, 100–102, 110, 111, 115, 140, 142, 144, 163, 164, 169–171
  classroom, 161
  deliberative, 92, 95
  democratic, 9
  educational, 35, 97
    democratic, 101
  hostile, 92, 93
  human (*see* Human, encounters)
  online, 164–170
  pedagogical, 2, 8, 22 (*see also* Pedagogical encounters)
  responsive, xiii
  sceptical, 76, 77
Engagement, ix, xi, xiii, xx, 5, 9, 16–19, 21, 22, 31, 33, 36, 40, 44, 48, 50, 52, 54, 58, 59, 65, 66, 68, 77, 82, 85,

87, 89, 91, 92, 94, 95, 97, 101, 111, 117–119, 141, 145–147, 149, 160, 164, 167
  communal, 94
  community of, 134
  critical, 68, 110, 162
  cultural, 117
  in debate, 132
  deliberative, 45, 61, 116–118, 133, 149, 150
  deliberative democratic, 34
  democratic, 110
  evocatively, 1
  internal, 153
  online, 167–169
  pedagogic, 10
  political, 10
  provocative, 149
  reasonable, 117
  respectfully, 66
  student, 161
Engaging relationships, *see* Relationships, engaging
Entities
  autonomous, 20
Equal/equality, vi, 18, 19, 32, 56–58, 82, 91, 102, 106, 130, 134, 142, 143, 145, 146, 152
  attain, 147
  citizens, 132, 146, 151, 155
  claim, 146
  demand, 146
  exercise of, 107
  gender, 130–132, 136, 143
  gendered view, 129
  intellectual, 145, 155
  intelligence, 18, 19, 58, 91, 145–148, 152
  method of, 19
  pursuit of, 106
  of speech, 19
  of voice, 144, 154
Ethnic/ethical
  actions, 108
  beings, xiii, 28, 108
  concerns, 94
  conflict, 94, 118
  care/caring, 36, 114 (*see also* Care/caring, ethical)
  conciliation, 7
  differences, 90
  imperative, 28
  privileges, 122
  of relation, 13
  responsibility, 26, 29–32, 34, 36, 59, 61, 105–110
  of ubuntu, xviii, 90, 91
Ethic of care, v, x, xi, xvii–xx, 2–11, 15, 29, 35, 36, 40, 42, 43, 49, 65, 90, 102, 110, 114, 129, 147–149, 151, 155, 170
  ubuntu, 90, 91
Exclusion, 4, 5, 9, 10, 35, 43, 78, 93–95, 122, 125, 131–134, 136–139, 141, 143, 145, 167
  attitudes, 140
  exclusionary practices, 129, 144, 147
  external, 9, 134, 142
  forms of, 133, 137, 140, 141
  groups, 146–150
  internal, xix, 10, 129, 133–142, 144, 145, 148, 150–155

new forms of, 133
permanent, 79, 80
political, 93
practices, 140, 152
social, 131
temporary, 78
women, xix, 132, 135–137
Experiences, v, xi, xix, xx, 2, 4, 10, 25, 28, 30, 53, 61, 74, 82, 123, 125, 133, 136–140, 142, 144, 164
   of African higher education, 129
   care, 107
   common, 58
   decolonial, 123, 125
   emotion, 150
   freedom, 73
   in higher education, 141, 163
   human, xii, 1, 28, 40
   humanity, 147
   inclusion, 78
   inclusive human, 1
   of internal exclusion, 141
   interrelated human, 1
   learning, 9, 79, 161
   life, 120
   lived, 154
   misfortune, 150
   moments of internal exclusion, 129
   of others, 75, 123
   pedagogical, xiii
   practical, 79
   pragmatic, 36
   of reflective openness, 84
   relational, 9, 72
   students, 76, 102, 161, 170
   transactional, 39
   unsatisfactory, 140
   vulnerabilities, 46, 150
   women's, 137, 140
   world of, 18, 58
Exploitation, 29, 93
Express, xxi, 4, 18, 19, 27, 59, 125, 152

F

Faculty of education, 26, 53
Fallibility, 42, 43, 47, 101
   of students, 47
Fear, 27, 28, 51, 139, 141, 165
   of intimidation, 142
Feminine
   roles, 143
Forgiveness, 63, 92
Freedom, 27, 28, 30, 32, 33, 56, 73, 94, 106, 107
   academic, 93
   pursuit of, 106
   of speech, 68, 91
Free speech, *see* Speech, free
Freire, Paulo, v, xvi, 22, 26–32, 36, 39, 55, 108, 130
Freirean
   approach, 31
   notion, 30, 31
   notion of caring, 32
   tradition, 35

G

Gender, 35, 67, 68, 129–132, 135, 142, 144, 145, 147, 149, 155
   differences, 133

divide, 148, 153
equality, 130
gap, 135
inequality, 132, 134–136
perspective of, 143
relations, 144

H

Higher education, v, vii, xv, xvi, xviii, 2, 4, 26, 31, 32, 39, 51, 61, 86, 97, 99, 100, 105–107, 109, 113, 114, 116, 119, 121, 126, 127, 129, 131, 132, 134–143, 145–147, 153, 155, 163–165
  access to, 134, 136
  Africa, 129
  African, 129–132
Higher learning, 86, 93
  institutions of, 68, 107, 113
Hopeful, 28, 33
Human, xii, xiii, xv, xvi, xix, 1–7, 10, 11, 18, 28, 29, 41, 43, 77, 78, 82, 83, 92, 102, 106, 117, 120, 122, 126, 144, 147, 152
  act, xii
  actions, xv, 8, 11, 18, 95, 120, 122, 123, 127
  activity, 118
  adversity, 109
  attachments, 4, 8, 11
  beings, 8, 11, 91, 109, 137, 145, 147, 148, 150–153, 169
  capacity, 148–149
  capital, 136
  condition, 28, 82, 121
  conflict, 90
  development, 33
  dignity, 67
  embodiment, 123
  emotion, 74
  empowerment, 33
  encounters, xv, 5, 18, 89, 101, 108, 110, 117
  engagement, 9, 117
  exclusion, 31
  experience, xii, 40
  fallibilism, 42, 50
  fallibility, 43
  flourishing, 50
  freedoms, 95
  injustice, 94
  intellectual fallibility, 48
  interconnectedness, 76
  interdependence, 3, 89, 90, 92
  interrelationships, 2, 11, 41, 123
  life, 20, 60, 119
  living, 108
  misery, 29
  mode of action, 27
  persons, 114
  practices, 108
  prosperity, 86
  relations, 75, 86, 149
  relationships, 3, 95
  resources, 103
  responsibility, 11
  self, 89
  solidarities, 84
  suffering, 31
  trafficking, 86, 94, 108, 119
  vulnerability, 84
Humane virtues, xviii, 90

Humanity, vi, 30, 31, 35, 36, 77, 80, 82, 84, 90, 92, 101, 108–110, 121, 122, 126, 127, 130, 147, 151–155
  act of, 121
  crimes against, 109
Humanness, 3, 91, 95
  sense of, 89
Humiliation, 94
  public, 109

Ideas
  autonomous, 72
  politico-educational, 27
  transformative, 27
Identities, 41, 127, 165, 166, 168
Inattentive, 51, 59, 60, 71, 105
Inclusion, 9, 11, 33, 47, 56, 71, 78, 98, 106, 130–134, 137, 140, 143, 145–147, 152, 153, 155
  authenticity of, 2
  democratic (*see* Democracy, inclusion)
  external, 129
  gender-based, 142–144, 147
  genuine, 131
  internal, 10, 140, 142–144, 147–149, 152, 153
  justified, 133
  moments of, 80
  practice of, 8
  substantive, 132, 140, 144, 155
  surface, 140
  vigorous, 146
  ways of, 132
Inclusive, xvi, 1, 3, 5, 10, 11, 13, 39, 42, 56, 61, 71, 114, 132, 137, 145, 147, 154
  caring, 4, 5, 11
  democratic processes, 133
  democratic society, 131
  processes, 133
Inclusiveness
  relationship of, 3
Inhumanity, 90, 110
Injustice, 34, 41, 51, 67, 84, 86, 94, 95, 110, 119, 121, 152, 154, 168
  epistemic, 119
  forms of, 150
  social, 35
  societal, 95
Inquiry
  deliberative, 34, 95, 116, 126
Institutions, vi, 43, 65, 93, 107, 113, 133, 136, 137, 147
  African, 131
  AHE, 155
  democratic, 146, 153
  democratic AHE, 155
  educational, xviii, 31, 95, 131
  equal, 137
  higher, 143
  higher education, xix
  of higher learning, 68, 93, 107, 113
  male-dominated, 138
  of society, 132
  social, 67, 134, 143, 146
Integrity, 2, 91

Intellectual
  advances, 53
  adventure, 19
  challenge, 33
  concerns, 19
  credibility, 104
  development, 154
  discussion, 166
  encounters, 169
  equality, 19, 57, 145–147, 155
  error, 47
  fallibility, 48
  programmes, 31
  projects, 31
  pursuits, 95, 106
  rigor, 66
  rigour, 48
  risks, 153
  skills, 147
  standards, 66
  work, 31, 35, 63
Intelligence
  equal (*see* Equal/equality, intelligence)
Interconnectedness, 11, 76, 89, 90, 151
Intolerance, 67

Judgement
  autonomous, xiv
  emotional, 150
  evaluative, xii
  practical, 47
  premature, 76
  rational, xiv, 2, 56
Justice, vi, xii, xiii, xv, xvii, 29, 32, 35, 51, 56, 58, 61, 63, 66–69, 83, 84, 86, 90, 102, 106, 108, 118, 127, 146, 152
  actions for, 95
  communal, 34, 35
  educational, 63
  epistemic, 118–121, 126
  pursuit of, 106
  social, 33
  ubuntu, 90
Justification, 6, 14, 56, 59
  of equality, 143

K

Knowledge, 17, 20, 32, 41, 42, 51, 53, 74, 132, 135–137, 167
  acquisition of, 51
  commodification of, 99
  production, 136

L

Language
  Afrikaans, 27
  of oppression, 27
  power of, 145
  proficiency, 142
  theoretical, 116
  use of, 134
Leadership, 104
  capacity, 103
  philosophy, 41
  positions, 41, 137, 138
Learning, v–vii, xi, xiii, xix, 1, 2, 9, 16, 31, 32, 35, 42, 44, 46, 51, 57, 77, 80, 84, 85, 87, 116, 117, 164–167
  assessments for, 162

attentiveness to, 28
authentic, xiii, 36, 117
autonomous, 77
blended, 167
critical, 166
experience of, 79
management systems, 161
needs, 161
rote, 32, 47, 164, 165
student, 1
supportive, 44
transactional, 42
Life, 32, 83, 118, 120, 126
academic, 2
challenges of, 26
day-to-day, 115
experiences, 120
force, 114, 115
human, 20, 60, 119
public, 33
quality of, 114, 126
self-managed, 32
skills, 115
university, 115
worlds, 116
Loyalty, 83, 84
reflective, 84, 85

M

Marginalised/marginalisation, 27, 43, 45, 67, 94, 106, 131, 148
groups, 145, 147
peoples, 27, 67
Meanings, xiii, 16, 22
alternative, 16
of things, 51
underlying, 94
Modelling, 14–22

Moral/morality, 41, 90
cause, 83
education, 13, 14, 17
notion of, 114
point of view, 20
respect, 90
sensitivity, 66
solidarity, 83
standards, 66
Muslim, x, 42, 43, 51, 120
architecture, 124
Mutual criticism
atmosphere of, 4
Mutuality, xii, xvi, 40

N

Narratives, 68, 98, 101
women, 137
Neo-Freirean scholars, 30
Non-democracy, 71
Non-empathy, 71, 76
Non-inclusion, 71, 78–80
Non-inclusive, 78
Non-pragmatism, 71
Nonviolence, 3
premise of, 3
relationship of, 4

O

Openness, 9, 27, 81, 83, 94, 103, 107, 110, 123, 164
reflective, 84, 85
reflexive, 84
Opportunity, 22, 53, 54, 57, 59, 68, 90, 95, 99, 115, 117, 135, 137, 140, 161–163, 169
equal, 9, 11, 35, 57, 115, 137

Oppression, 67, 108, 122
Otherness, xix, 50, 83, 84, 87, 102
Others, 151–153
   dominant, 109, 152, 154

P

Patience, 31, 105
Pedagogical
   approach, 15, 16
   atmosphere, 47
   authentication, 21
   authority, 46, 56
   autonomy, 56
   concerns, xiii, xv, 59
   engagements, 170
   forgiveness, 92
   intimacy, 68, 69
   narratives, 31
   opportunity, 15
   possibility, 21
   practices, xiii, 166
   relations, xviii, 7, 21, 61, 117
   relationships, xvi, 15, 63
   work, 159
Pedagogical encounters, v, vi, xi, xiii–xix, 1, 2, 5, 7–11, 15, 21, 22, 28, 30, 32, 34, 36, 39, 43, 45, 46, 48, 49, 51–54, 56, 58, 61, 63–67, 69, 71, 72, 74–87, 89, 91, 92, 95, 99, 108, 110, 113, 114, 117, 126, 145, 152, 155, 159, 161, 168, 170
   belligerent, 8
   disruptive, 77
   dissonant, 159
   distressful, 8
   inclusive, xvi
   intellectual, 169
   online, 170
   rigorous, 77
   sceptical, 77
Pedagogy, vii, xvii, xix, 15, 27, 33, 54, 105–110, 114–116, 127, 159–161
   critical, v, xvi, 30, 32, 36
   embodied, 114, 115
   of the oppressed, 26, 27
Philosophical tradition, 114, 127
Philosophy
   of education, ix, x, xii, xix, xx, xxvii, 3–5, 9, 14, 16, 34, 35, 44, 45, 82, 85, 117–119
      African, 3–5, 35, 36, 82, 85, 86, 117
      indigenous African, 3
   of higher education, xviii, 113, 114, 116–119, 122, 126, 127
   of teaching, 116
Point of view, 4, 66, 151
   autonomous, xiv
   independent, xiv
   moral, 20
Political
   actions, 108
   activist, 27
   awareness, 27, 29, 30
   practices, 129
   subjugation, 94

Positivism, 59
Positivistic
　inquiry, 59
Post-apartheid, 4, 33
　era, 34
　university education, 34
Post-colonial, 94, 120, 133
　democratic institutions, 146
Post-colonialism, 93
Potentialities, xi, xvi, xx, 2, 26, 28, 65, 78, 81, 154
　rational, 149
　of students and teachers, 2
Power
　relationship, 144, 152
　　dominant, 144
Practical/practicality, v, xiv, xvi, xviii, 11, 13–15, 20, 22, 39, 42, 61, 71, 79, 82, 126, 162
　caring, xvi, 11, 13–15, 22
Practice, ix, xvi, xx, 4, 8, 14, 27, 28, 31, 36, 46, 49, 56, 64, 65, 100, 108, 110, 116, 125, 127, 164, 166
　of caring, 20
　educative, 29
　enabling, 105
　of freedom, 32
　of justice, 84
　of pragmatic caring, 45
　of scepticism, 75
Pragmatic, xvi, 36, 41–47, 71, 84
Prejudice, 29, 75, 137
　remarks, 142
Presence
　condition of, 74

Q

Questions, vi, 14, 99, 142, 148, 165, 167
　objective-type, 162
　probing, 168
Quran, 42
　recitation, 42, 43

R

Race/racism/racist, 4, 34, 35, 68, 94, 110, 122, 130, 132, 135
Rationality, xii, 14, 111
　African, 118
　deliberative, 44
　limited, 150
Reason, xviii, 32, 130
Reasonableness, 9, 14
Reasoning abilities, 149, 154
Recognition, xx, 10, 11, 13, 14, 20–22, 40, 43, 45, 48, 77, 90, 92, 95, 107, 108, 116, 120, 123, 166
　mutual, 21
　of vulnerability, 151
Reconcile, 92
Reconciliation, 63, 67, 91, 109
Reflect, xvii, 16, 30, 65, 83, 119, 139, 144, 152, 169, 170
　empathically, 67
　willingness to, 49, 50
Relational act, 6, 148
Relationality, xvi, 5, 6, 10, 11, 39, 55, 114
　act of (see Act, relationality)
Relations
　positive, 14

Index

Relationship
  care/caring, x, 9, 22, 148, 155 (*see also* Care/caring, relationships of)
  of connection, 2
  cosmopolitan, 84
  dyadic, 61
  engaging, 7
  hierarchical, 56, 57
  intersubjective, 21
  pedagogical, 165 (*see also* Pedagogical, relationships)
  transactional, 50, 77
Research
  disciplinary, 114
  educational, ix, x, 2, 59, 102, 104, 105, 107, 109
  excellence, 104
  productivity, 104–106
Respect, xvii, 11, 21, 28, 35, 42, 47, 63, 66, 67, 69, 78, 89, 95, 114, 143, 145, 151, 153
  compassionate, 149
  equal, 10
  for individuals, 65
  mutual, xv
  worthy of, 67
Respectful, 11, 21, 92
Responsibility, xiii, 7, 9–11, 29, 33, 46, 55, 78, 92, 101, 105, 116, 118–121, 126, 151–155, 168
  human (*see* Human, responsibility)
  political, 61
  taking, 151
Responsiveness, xvi, 43, 46
Restoration, 90

Rhythm, vi, vii, xi, xiv, xv, xvii, xviii, 60, 71–81, 86, 87, 89, 92, 97, 99–102, 105–111, 113, 161, 162, 164, 166, 168–170
  account of, 73
  action, xi, 74
  caring, 159
  dances, 101
  presence of, 73
Right
  of belonging to humanity, 90
Roles, 97, 108, 140, 152, 165
  feminine, 143
  gendered, 144
  important, 162
  masculine, 143
  and responsibilities, vi
  socially constructed, 144
  as students, 167
  valuable, 163

Scepticism, vi, xiv, xvii, 71, 75–78, 80, 102, 159, 162, 168, 170
Scholarly, xii, 33, 53, 59, 103, 104, 108
  interests, 106
  work, 100
Scholarship, xi, 2, 55, 93, 94, 99, 103, 104, 106
  African, 4
  black, 4, 99
  enhanced, 104
  meaningful, 113
  university, 109
Self-confidence, 20, 139

Self-esteem, 20, 137
  lowering, 139
Self-reflection, 32, 152
Self-respect, 20
Self, the, xiv, xvii, 20, 51, 89, 123, 142, 150–152
Self-understandings, xiii
Showing, 14–22, 90, 107, 123
  respect, 151
Social
  constructs, 144
  development, 131
  institutions, 67, 134, 143, 146, 154
  justice, 155, 168
  power, 144
  practices, 18, 129
Societal
  concerns, 109
Socio-economic
  backgrounds, 140
  concerns, 94
  status, 140
Solidarity, 28, 31, 35, 60, 83, 114, 126, 127
South Africa, 4, 26, 58, 61, 98, 106, 109, 135–137, 140, 141, 164–166
Speaking beings, 18, 19, 57
  equal, 18, 20
Speech, xiii, xviii, xx, 6, 11, 19, 57, 69, 91
  acts, 9, 48
  authentic, xiii
  discriminatory, 68
  free, 56
  harmful, 68
  injurious, 63, 68
  provocative, 68, 69

unjust, 69
Status, 19, 53, 73, 99, 129, 130, 134, 153
  flagship, 94
  marital, 74
  quo, 107, 148, 154
  socio-economic, 140
  subordinate, 139
Students, v, vi, ix, xii–xiv, xvi, xviii, xx, 1, 5–7, 9–11, 14, 15, 17, 19, 21, 22, 26–33, 35, 43, 44, 46, 47, 50–53, 56–58, 60, 61, 64–69, 72, 76–82, 84–87, 91, 92, 94, 95, 101, 102, 108, 110, 111, 114–117, 119, 123, 126, 132, 136, 137, 140, 141, 147–150, 153, 154, 159–163, 165–170
  arguments, 169
  autonomous, 65
  female, 134, 135, 140, 141, 143
  needs, 168
  post-graduate, 44, 60
  supervision, 21, 97
  university, 166, 169, 170
  unquestioning, 15
  and teachers, 1, 21, 22, 33, 34, 43, 57, 68, 77, 87
Suffering, 28, 29, 33, 150, 151
  listening to, 109
Supervisor, v, xviii, 60, 97, 142
Sympathy, xv, 41, 64–66

Teachers, vi, xii–xvi, xviii, xix, 1, 5, 7, 10, 11, 15, 16, 19, 21, 22, 26, 28, 29, 32, 33, 35,

43, 47, 50, 52, 53, 56–58, 61, 65–69, 76, 78, 81, 84–87, 91, 94, 116, 126, 153, 160, 162, 167, 168
socially conscious, 168
and students, xvi, xvii, 7, 8, 15, 20–22, 28–30, 33, 34, 44–48, 51–53, 56, 57, 77, 80, 84–87, 91, 92, 94, 95, 114, 115
Teaching, xiii, xvi, xviii, 1, 2, 15, 30, 31, 33, 43, 44, 52, 56, 65, 77, 79, 80, 82, 86, 94, 107, 110, 114, 116, 160, 161, 164–167
  act of, 1
  approach, 16
  authentic, 27
  authoritative, 36
  emancipatory method of, 145
  and learning, xvi, xviii, 1, 2, 15, 16, 31, 52, 77, 86, 90, 104, 107, 110, 114–116, 160, 161, 167
    African, 89
    embodied, 117
    expectations, 160
    interrelationship of, 1
    pedagogy of, 15
    practices, 94
    requirement, 160
  methods, 113
  pedagogic act of, 15
  quality, 104
  time, 161
  understanding of, 28
Technology/technological competency, 167
educational, 159–167
Theoretical, v
  carelessness, 117
  dead zone, 116
  discourse, 117
  enhancement, 117
  framework, vii
  ideas, 72, 74
  insights, 99
  landscape, v
  language, 116
  reflection, 44
  rigorous, 28, 102
  views, 72
  views on caring, xvi
Theory, 41
  of the community, 21
  democratic, xx
  of democratic inclusion, 10
  of education, 72, 82 (*see also* Education, theories)
  pictorial, 16, 17
  picture, 16
  social democratic, xx
  of understanding, 82
Think/thinking, 20, 101, 119
  autonomous, 93
  boundaries of, vii
  capacity for, 58
  about care, x, xxi
  caringly, 114
  critical, 145
  deeper, 16
  about democracy, xx
  about equality, 145
  of others, 10
  and practices, 30
  on rhythm, xi, 114

routine, 166
about the self, 142
for themselves, 29, 54, 58, 65
voluntary, 145
Transactional, xvi, 36, 39, 42–45, 47, 48, 50, 61
Transformation, 4, 59, 99, 103, 105–110, 171
educational, 59
legitimate, 142
Trust, 10, 11, 21, 43, 53, 68, 69, 110
mutual, 11, 21
relationship of, 60
Truth, 7, 32, 109
incomplete, 16
pursuit of, 123

U

Ubuntu, v, 3, 87, 89–93, 114
African ethic of, 87, 90
care/caring, xviii, 90–95
education, 90
ethic of, 91
ethic of care, 91 (*see* Ethic of care, ubuntu)
justice, 86, 90
notion of, 92
orientation, 89
practice, 90
sense of, 168
Uncaring, 40
relationships, 153
Unconditionality, 124, 125
Undermine, 4, 26, 29, 61, 67, 90, 108, 126, 129, 136, 144

Understandings, xiii, xv, xvi, xix, xxi, 2, 8, 18, 19, 22, 31, 44, 45, 74, 82, 101, 161, 162
alternative, 15–17
autonomous, 47
care/caring, 64, 71
independent, 17
local, 118
University teachers, 1, 10, 15, 19, 21, 34, 47, 66, 94, 95, 160, 161, 167

V

Views, xiv, xv, 10, 55, 56, 68, 76, 149, 168
on an African philosophy of education, 5, 9
alternative, 48
autonomous, 17
belligerent, 68
on caring, xvi
of Carol Gilligan, xvi
controversial, 68
on cosmopolitanism, xviii
on education, 85
initial, 5
multiple, xv
of one another, 85
on pedagogical encounters, 170
previously held, 107
of students, 43, 76
of teachers, xiv
theoretical, 72
unjustifiable, 44
Violation, 4
Violence, 5, 40, 84, 91, 108, 110

Voices, vii, x, 2, 6, 60, 131, 133, 134, 136, 137, 139, 142–146, 148, 149, 151–153, 155, 166
  assertion of, 145–147
  autonomous, 95
  citizens, 56
  critical, 30
  different, 5
  equalisation of, 129, 147, 149
  equality of, 145
  of the excluded, 145
  missing, 41
  own, 4, 153
  student, 152, 167
  women's, 138, 142, 153
Vulnerabilities, 46, 90, 92, 125, 149, 151

W

Wisdom, 51, 66
Women, 41, 67, 106, 129–142, 144, 146, 147, 149, 152, 153, 155
  academic, 139
  access, 134, 136
  access to university education, 131
  activists, 40
  African, 146, 153
  on the African continent, xix, 129
  in AHE, 148
  dependent, 131
  empowerment, 130
  equal access, 134
  excluded, 136
  exclusion, 132, 133, 135, 136, 153
  experiences, 129, 137, 139, 140
  in higher education, 131
  inclusion, 131
  independence, 42
  integrity, 2
  internal exclusion, xix, 129, 142
  internal inclusion, 153
  in leadership positions, 138
  mature, 141
  men and, 3, 140, 143, 147, 154
  narratives, 137
  need, 139
  other, 2, 141
  passive, 131
  percentages of, 135
  physical representation, 142
  position of, 146
  presence, 133
  resistance, 139
  role models, 138
  in senior positions, 138
  sense of integrity, 2
  single, 142
  in society, 140
  space for, 134
  statistics of, 135
  struggle, 137
  as students, 136, 137
  as subordinate citizens, 152
  subordinate status, 139
  voices, 138, 142, 144, 153
Writing, ix, xi, xii, xix, xx, 2, 16, 21, 26, 31, 58, 64, 90, 98, 100, 102, 106, 108, 111, 164
  group, 163
  for profit, 108
  for recognition, 108
  skills, 163

Printed in the United States
By Bookmasters